Positive Th

Days

Practical Workbook to Think Positive; Train your Inner
Critic, Stop Overthinking and Change your Mindset

(Become a Mindful and Positive Person)

MASTER.TODAY

Roger Reed

The Journey of a thousand miles begins with a single step.

-Lao Tzu

Introduction

What do you think about when you hear the term *"positive thinking?"* Do you imagine thinking positively means being upbeat all the time? Or does it make you think about a quasi-mystical approach through which sending positive thoughts will somehow bring health, wealth, and contentment?

Both of those assumptions are misapprehensions. Positive thinking is about learning to focus on the good in any given situation. It doesn't mean making light of setbacks or problems. It does not mean that you will be happy all the time, and it certainly doesn't mean ignoring reality. It means approaching everything you do with the expectation that the outcome will be positive. That doesn't sound very complicated or difficult, but it's actually much more challenging than most people think. Many of us are conditioned to be negative, to fear the worst rather than expecting the best. We may not even be aware of this tendency, but that attitude can permeate everything we do.

Learning to expect the best in any situation probably doesn't sound very impressive, so why should you care about positive thinking? A number of scientific studies have found remarkable links between positive thinking and improvements in both physical and mental health. For example, a 2006 study[1] of several hundred people was carried out by Professor Sheldon Cohen and a team of researchers from Carnegie Mellon University in Pennsylvania. They found that those test subjects with a PES (Positive Emotional Style) were significantly more resistant when they were exposed to a virus. It wasn't just that these people were less likely to report adverse symptoms. Careful measurements confirmed that somehow, people who were positive thinkers were better able to fight off infection. The study concluded that:

> *"These results indicate that PES may play a more important role in health than previously thought."*

---

[1] Sheldon Cohen, Cuneyt M Alper, William J Doyle, John J Treanor, Ronald B Turner, *Positive emotional style predicts resistance to illness after experimental exposure to rhinovirus or influenza virus*, Journal of Psychosomatic Medicine, November 2006.

Other studies agree and indicate that, in addition to improved resistance to infection, being a positive thinker also significantly lowers your chances of suffering from high blood pressure, having a heart attack, gives you superior resistance to pain, and may even lead to an increased life span. The idea that positive thinking can make you live longer may sound like an extravagant claim, but it, too is backed-up by studies. In one study started in the 1930s by researchers from the University of Kentucky[2], a group of young Catholic nuns were asked to write short autobiographies. Startlingly, the nuns whose written accounts provided positive emotional content lived, on average, 10 years longer than those who showed negative emotional content! That's a more notable improvement than attained by adopting a healthier lifestyle through, for example, giving up smoking!

Improved physical health and longevity alone are good reasons to learn how to think positively, but positive thinking also provides profound improvements in mental health. It is unsurprising that positive thinking is directly linked with a reduction in depression, anxiety, and suicidal thoughts. What is less well-known is that positive thinking is also associated with improved creativity, greater problem-solving skills, and higher probability of adopting a healthy lifestyle.

Barbara Fredrickson, Ph.D., is the Kenan Distinguished Professor at the University of North Carolina at Chapel Hill and the Director of the university's Positive Emotions and Psychophysiology (PEP) Laboratory. In an interview for the *BeWell* Program at Stanford University, she said:

> *"We are learning that positive emotions act like nutrients. While experiences of joy, gratitude, or serenity may seem fleeting and inconsequential, science is showing that these experiences*

---

[2] Deborah D. Danner, David A. Snowdon, and Wallace V. Friesen, *Positive Emotions in Early Life and Longevity: Findings from the Nun Study*, University of Wisconsin, 2001.

influence how our brains work, opening our mindsets to become more encompassing and flexible.[3]"

These studies and continuing research make it clear that while learning positive thinking won't guarantee you wealth or instant success, it will make you healthier, allow you to live longer, and improve mental wellbeing. Positive thinking isn't an innate ability, something that you are born with. It is a set of skills and techniques that can be learned by anyone, no matter their current state of mind. This book will teach you how to become a positive thinker.

Are you ready to learn positive thinking and to change your life for the better?

---

[3] *The power of positive emotions*, retrieved from https://bewell.stanford.edu/the-power-of-positive-emotions/, May 2021.

YOUR FREE GIFT

Subscribe to our mailing list and get instant access to "**5 Quick Tips to Develop more Discipline & Willpower**"

We would like to give you a gift to thank you for purchasing this book. You can choose from any of our other published titles.

You can get immediate access to any of our books by clicking on the link below and joining our mailing list:

https://campsite.bio/mastertoday

Our other books

Mental Toughness & Discipline Mastery: *Build your Self-Confidence to Unlock your Courage and Resilience*

Find out more here:

https://master.today/books/mental-toughness/

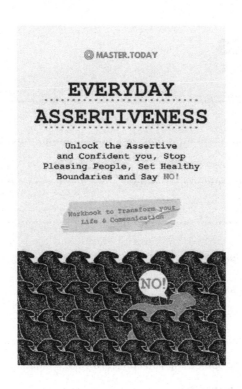

Everyday Assertiveness: *Unlock the Assertive and Confident you, Stop Pleasing People, Set Healthy Boundaries and Say NO!*

(Workbook to Transform your Life & Communication)

Find out more here:

https://master.today/books

Contents

Chapter 1: What is Positive Thinking?

This chapter introduces the main ideas behind positive thinking. We explain what it is, and, perhaps just as important, what it isn't. There is good scientific evidence that shows that positive thinking can dramatically improve your physical and mental health, but some approaches use this term to denote something mystical and not confirmed by science.

Are you a positive thinker?

Before we discuss how to adopt the habits of positive thinking, we need to determine what positive habits are.

In his book *The Emotional Life of Your Brain*[4], the founder of the Center of Healthy Minds at the University of Wisconsin-Madison Dr. Richard J. Davidson, cites neuroscientific evidence to support his claim that our personalities result from a combination of just six emotional styles:

- **Resilience** refers to how well an individual deals with and recovers from adversity.
- **Outlook** refers to the ability of an individual to maintain a positive attitude towards the future.
- **Social intuition** is about how well a person recognizes non verbal cues during interaction with others.
- **Self-awareness** refers to the ability to be aware of one's own emotions and of physical sensations and signals.
- **Sensitivity to context** is about how appropriately a person's emotional and behavioral responses take into account a situation's context.
- **Attention** is the ability to remain focused and to ignore distractions.

Emotional styles are different to emotional states. An emotional style represents an overall pattern of emotional responses. An emotional state is a transitory emotional response to a particular situation. For example, your emotional state following a setback or disappointment may be unhappiness, but your overall emotional style may remain positive.

Within each of the six emotional styles identified by Davidson, a person tends to be either positive or negative. People who generally score highly in all six categories are said to have a Positive Emotional Style (PES). People who score less highly are said to have a Negative Emotional Style

---

[4] Richard J Davidson Ph.D, Sharon Begley, *The Emotional Life of Your Brain: How Its Unique Patterns Affect the Way You Think, Feel, and Live--And How You Can Change Them*, Avery Publishing Group, 2012

(NES). A number of studies strongly suggest that we can modify our emotional styles through deliberate, systematic training.

Do you have a PES or an NES? Most of intuitively know whether we tend to the positive or the negative, but sometimes it can be helpful to assess our emotional patterns objectively.

To do this, think honestly about how you would answer the following questions about your own emotional styles:

> **Resilience.** Do you respond positively to setbacks and problems? Do you recover quickly from a setback? If something goes wrong, is it likely that you will try the same thing again?

> **Outlook.** Is your view of the future generally positive? Do you look forward to the day when you get up in the morning?

> **Social intuition.** Are you aware of how people feel even when they don't directly speak about those feelings? Have you ever been aware of how another person is feeling even though other people don't seem to notice?

> **Self-awareness.** Do you easily understand how and why people respond to your actions? Are you generally aware of your own emotions? Are you generally aware of your body and the physical sensations you experience?

> **Sensitivity to context.** Do you intuitively understand how to behave appropriately in most circumstances? Do you notice when other people behave in socially inappropriate ways?

> **Attention.** Are you good at staying focused? Are you generally able to maintain concentration on a task until it is complete?

This is by no means a complete assessment of your emotional styles, but if you can generally answer "*Yes*" to most of these questions, you probably have a PES. If you generally answer "*No*," then you may have an NES. If you would like to try a more detailed emotional style test, there are several available on-line. One of the best, developed with the assistance of Dr. Richard Davidson, can be found on the University of Wisconsin-Madison website:

The fact that you are reading this book suggests you are interested in learning how to change an NES to a PES. This book will help you to do that, by showing you how to adopt the habits of positive thinking. However, emotional styles are often not consistent across all realms of our lives. For example, you may be generally positive and optimistic in terms of your personal relationships but you may find yourself struggling with negativity at work.

For that reason, you may want to assess yourself more than once, answering the questions for different parts of your life or in the different roles that you play (parent, colleague, friend, partner, etc.). Be as specific as possible when identifying the areas where a lack of positive thinking is holding you back.

When you are happy that you understand your current situation, you may want to try the first exercise in Chapter 9, *Your positive thinking assessment*.

What are the benefits of positive thinking?

The fact that positive thinking and developing a PES have a direct benefit for physical health is now generally accepted by most health practitioners. So many studies confirm this that is has become undeniable. What is less clear is why There are many theories about why positive thinking makes us healthier and allows us to live longer, but the most generally accepted is that positive thinking reduces stress.

Stress is how we react to situations that we perceive as hazardous. Stress is not in itself harmful. In short bursts, it triggers our *"fight or flight"* response, helping us \void the hazard. Stress becomes a problem when it is always present. This is known as *"chronic stress."* In the modern world, many of us balance conflicting demands on our time and attention. We feel pulled in different directions, and there never seems to be enough time to do everything properly. Chronic stress has a number of direct physical effects. These include but are not limited to:

- **High blood pressure**
- **Racing heart**
- Over time, high blood pressure and a racing heart can lead to an **increased risk of a heart-attack**
- **Shortness of breath**
- **Weakened immune system**
- **High blood sugar**, making you more prone to Type 2 diabetes
- **Reduced sex-drive**
- Tense muscles, leading to **headaches and back and shoulder aches**

Chronic stress is also directly associated with issues of mental health. It can lead to problem behaviors such as overeating, not eating enough, drug abuse, a lack of exercise, and alcohol abuse. It can cause insomnia and mood disorders such as anxiety, irritability, and even depression.

Many of us get so used to living with stress every day that we no longer even notice it. Nevertheless, chronic stress makes you unhealthy and unhappy and will almost certainly mean that you won't live as long as you otherwise might.

You could remove stress by completely changing your life to avoid the pressures that cause it. You could give up your job, quit your relationships, and go live in the countryside. For most people, however, that is not a viable option because it requires a fundamental change to your life and work. It is important to remember that stress is not an inescapable part of a busy and productive life. Stress is not about the world around you. It is about how you perceive and react to that world.

Positive thinking will not remove the factors that cause stress in your life. However, it will change the way that you interpret those things reducing the effects of stress and all the physical and mental problems it causes. That alone is a good reason to learn the techniques of positive thinking, but the benefits don't stop there.

Becoming a positive thinker will improve your personal and professional relationships. If that sounds unlikely, think of the people you enjoy spending time with. How many of those are negative complainers who always seem to be miserable and unhappy? How many are positive, upbeat, and confident? The vast majority of people prefer to spend their time with someone who is optimistic. If you can become a positive thinker, you will also become the kind of person people want to spend time with.

Positive thinkers also succeed more often. There have been a number of studies that indicate that positive people not only have better relationships and careers, they also make more money. One meta-analysis of studies that covered more than 275,000[5] people concluded that:

> *"Numerous studies show that happy individuals are successful across multiple life domains, including marriage, friendship, income, work performance, and health. The happiness–success link exists not only because success makes people happy, but also because positive affect engenders success."*

---

[55] Sonja Lyubomirsky, Laura King, Ed Diener, *The Benefits of Frequent Positive Affect: Does Happiness Lead to Success?*, American Psychological Association, *Psychological Bulletin*, 2005.

In another study that looked at salespeople in the insurance business, those identified as optimistic earned on average 88% more than their pessimistic colleagues.

Positive thinking isn't just a vague belief that things will turn out well. It is a way of approaching life that will make you healthier, wealthier, and happier. This book shows you how to become a positive thinker and allow you to realize all those significant benefits.

Why is positive thinking so difficult?

More of us suffer from something called negativity bias, even though we don't recognize it. Experiencing negativity bias means that we are prone to focusing our mental and emotional energy on avoiding negative outcomes rather than pursuing positive outcomes. This bias probably began as a human survival mechanism. In humanity's earliest days, the world was a hazardous place and surviving meant constantly planning how to avoid dangers. For most of us in the modern world, questions of day-to-day survival are less pressing, but our brains are still focused on prioritizing this to avoid potentially negative events.

In neuroscience, the way in which we perceive things around us is called salience. Several psychological and cognitive science studies have shown that when the intensities of competing perceptions are equal, we tend to focus our attention on those that are, or have the potential to be, negative. In this way, salience exhibits a negativity bias.

This negativity bias may manifest in a number of ways, but the most common is accentuating the negative. Imagine that you have taken a test and scored 90%. Instead of celebrating the fact that you performed so well, negativity bias instead makes you irritated about missing out on that last 10%. Instead of being happy about your accomplishment, you are unhappy because you didn't do even better. A number of studies confirm this, tendency showing that:

- In relationships, it generally takes five good interactions to be perceived as counteracting a single bad interaction.
- People will generally put far more effort into avoiding losing money than into making the same amount of money.
- We remember painful and unpleasant experiences much more clearly than pleasant experiences.

As psychologist Rick Hanson, Ph.D., best-selling author[6] and Senior Fellow of UC Berkeley's Greater Good Science Center succinctly puts it:

---

[6] Rick Hansen, *Resilient: 12 Tools for transforming everyday experiences into lasting happiness*, Harmony, 2018

"It's safer for us to avoid sticks than it is to chase carrots."

Even our language reflects this. In virtually every language in the world, there are far more balanced and nuanced words and terms available to describe negative concepts[7]. This imbalance is especially noticeable in terms of emotions. The available vocabulary for describing negative feelings is generally much larger than that covering positive feelings, so perhaps this also makes it easier for us to dwell on the negative and dismiss the positive?

It seems that our brains are still attuned to the primitive needs of basic survival, leading us to giving more weight to avoiding harm than to pursuing the positive. To become a positive thinker, you must learn to overcome negativity bias.

---

[7] Paul Rozin, Loren Berman, Edward Royzman, *Biases in use of positive and negative words across twenty natural languages*, Cognition and Emotion, 2010.

Is positive thinking something you can learn?

We all experience a vast number of thoughts every day. Measuring a thought isn't easy, but most researchers claim that we experience between 12,000 and 60,000 thoughts each day. Due to negativity bias, it has been estimated that up to 80% of these thoughts are negative.

These statistics are frightening, but the good news is that they can be changed. We are all conditioned by our childhoods, environment, and the people we spend time with. Your mindset has been formed by a vast number of interrelated factors. However, your current mode of thinking is not fixed or inevitable.

Our brains develop neural pathways, short cuts that lead us to respond in the same way to external stimuli. For example, if you go for a drink after work to escape from stress, your brain will gradually develop a neural pathway telling you that the way to deal with stress is alcohol. Your brain will do so even when having a drink is neither appropriate nor possible. These mental short cuts lie behind many problem behaviors.

Recent developments in neuroscience tell us that these neural pathways are not fixed. If we want to change a behavior, all we need to do is to make a conscious decision to adopt the new behavior. If we can maintain that new behavior for a period of between 30 and 90 days, a new neural pathway will be formed. At that point, the new behavior becomes a habit and the old behavior is dropped.

In this book, we provide all the techniques you need to make positive thinking part of your life. If you make the effort to undertake these new behaviors, they will become habits. This will lead to the replacement of your current habits of negative thinking with new habits that support positive thinking.

What positive thinking isn't

The success of books such as *The Secret*[8] popularized the idea that positive thoughts bring positive results in some mysterious way. Followers of this concept cite what is called *The Law of Attraction.* According to this law, thoughts are regarded as a form of energy, and positive energy attracts health, finance, and relationship benefits

However, many neuroscientists and psychologists regard this notion as a pseudoscience. They claim that there is no basis for the semi-mystical belief that, by thinking positive thoughts you will somehow attract positive outcomes into your life through some unknown mechanism. That is not what this book is about.

This book is based entirely on science and psychology. It is based on the findings of a large number of studies published in peer-reviewed journals that confirm that positive thinking has notable physical and mental benefits. This book provides you with techniques you can use to become a positive thinker. There is no guarantee that using these will make you wealthy or attractive.

However, there is overwhelming scientific evidence that using the techniques outlined in this book will improve your ability to deal with stress, reduce your susceptibility to things like high blood pressure and heart attack, boost your immune system, and may even allow you to live longer. These techniques will also reduce anxiety and depression, boost your creativity and self-confidence, and make you better able to achieve your goals.

There is nothing mystical about positive thinking. There is nothing vague or mysterious about the benefits it brings. Using the techniques in this book may not make you rich, but they will improve your health and the quality of your life.

Are you ready to think positively?

---

[8] Rhonda Byrne, *The Secret*, Atria Books, 2006

Chapter 2: Overthinking

Overthinking is a common problem that causes distress and ill-health. Overthinking also blocks the use of the techniques of positive thinking. This chapter explains what overthinking is and how it may affect you.

What is overthinking?

Buddhist teaching has a wonderful analogy for intense, continuous thought from which many of us suffer. It calls this constant switching from one thought to another *"monkey mind."* Buddha described it in this way:

> *"Just as a monkey swinging through the trees grabs one branch and lets it go only to seize another, so too, that which is called thought, mind or consciousness arises and disappears continually both day and night.[9]"*

This analogy, also known as *kapicitta* in Buddhist teaching, describes perfectly how many of us react when we are stressed and constantly bombarded by information. We are easily distracted and unable to focus on any one thing.

We find yourselves constantly moving from one concerning thought to the next, unable to find resolution. We dwell on the past, especially on things we perceive as failures. We focus on the future, thinking about things we may do the next day, or week, or month. Ultimately, we lack focus where we really need it: On what we are doing right now.

Monkey mind is also associated with insomnia. We lie down, close our eyes and, instead of finding peace and tranquility, we find our minds racing. Our brains flit from thought to thought, leaving us feeling stressed and unable to sleep. The teachings of Buddha tell us that people have suffered from monkey mind for many thousands of years. However, in the modern world in which so many things clamor for a moment of our attention, suffering from monkey mind is even more common. Monkey mind is the enemy of positive thinking. You cannot be positive if your mind is constantly roaming from thought to thought. One of the techniques of positive thinking is learning to still the monkey mind, to find tranquility in focus.

In psychology, monkey mind is called overthinking. This thought pattern involves uncontrollable or intrusive thoughts that prevent you from

---

[99] Saṃyutta Nikāya, *The Connected Discourses of the Buddha*, trans. Bhikkhu Bodhi, Boston: Wisdom Publications, 2000

remaining focused on anything. It is often associated with obsessing about what may happen in the future or about past events. It often focuses on how you might have acted differently to produce a better outcome. Constantly replaying events from the past or trying to predict how future events may turn out is completely unproductive. You cannot change the past. You have a limited ability to control the future. You must learn instead to focus all your attention and energy on the present moment.

When overthinking becomes a problem

To a degree, we all overthink. The modern world can be a hectic place with competing demands on our time and attention. In this situation, it is a rare person who can remain tranquil all the time. Most people occasionally have trouble sleeping. This is often because they are worried about the past or the future.

Overthinking only becomes a serious problem when it is chronic, affecting you long-term. If you suffer from chronic overthinking, it impacts your ability to relate to other people and makes it difficult for you to function effectively each day. Overthinking leaves you stressed, tired, and focused on negative thoughts such as: *"Did I say the right thing?"* *"Will I look stupid at the meeting tomorrow?"*

When you just can't get things done because you are afraid of failing or repeating past mistakes, or when you can't focus on what you are doing because you are worrying about the past or future, overthinking can become a disorder that will affect everything you do. It can lead to anxiety and stress and it is associated with obsessive-compulsive disorder, and even depression.

Do you suffer from chronic overthinking?

The symptoms of overthinking

How can you tell if you are an overthinker? There are a number of physical and mental symptoms. If you suffer from these, you may be overthinking. Here are some of the main physical problems of overthinking:

> **Insomnia.** This is a classic symptom of overthinking, though not all insomnia is caused by overthinking. Do you find that when you try to sleep, that your mind suddenly begins racing? Do you seem to have no control over where it goes and end up feeling anxious, stressed, and unable to sleep?

> **Headaches.** Headaches have a range of causes. They can be a result of high blood pressure or a reaction to physical tension in the body. They can also have emotional causes, coming from stress, depression, and anxiety. Overthinking is a common cause of headaches. If you suffer from frequent headaches, overthinking may be the origin.

> **Muscle and joint pain.** When we are stressed or anxious, these emotions directly affect our body. We may tense muscles without realizing it, adopting odd postures. Maintaining this for any length of time causes muscle and joint pain. You may experience aching shoulders, neck, and back pain. If you suffer from these symptoms, they may be caused by overthinking.

> **Fatigue.** Lack of sleep, constant stress, and aches and pains are a drain on our energy. It is unsurprising that overthinking also leads to fatigue. If you find yourself constantly feeling tired, overthinking may be the cause.

In addition to physical symptoms, overthinking can also be recognized by patterns of thought. These are some of the most common mental processes associated with overthinking:

> **Anxiety.** Do you feel compelled to plan every future event down to the last detail? Do you find yourself worrying about future events? Do you suffer from free-floating anxiety, where you feel

anxious with no obvious cause? Do you ever use alcohol or drugs to reduce your feelings of anxiety? Some degree of anxiety is normal, especially if we are anticipating a difficult or challenging event. Constant anxiety is not normal and may be a symptom of overthinking.

Over analysis and fear of failure. How do you feel when you think about the future? Do you feel confident and calm? Or do you feel anxious, compelled to think through every possible scenario in exhaustive detail? Do you ever obsess about past events, analyzing them from every possible angle?" Have you ever avoided doing something because you are afraid that you won't perform well? Overthinking is often associated with a need to control the world around you. By analyzing the past and considering what may happen in the future, we imagine that we can shape that future to avoid failure. If you find yourself analyzing things in minute detail, you may be overthinking.

Failure to be in the present. What happened in the past cannot be changed. What may happen in the future is difficult to predict and impossible to completely control. The only part of your life where you exercise absolute control is the present instant. If your mind is concerned with the past or the "What if..." of the future, you cannot give all your energy and attention to what you are doing right now. The past is largely irrelevant, and the most effective way to shape the future is to do your best now. Overthinking makes us perform less effectively because it distracts us from the present moment.

Overthinking and GAD

Overthinking may be related to an underlying problem such as Generalized Anxiety Disorder (GAD). GAD is characterized by constant non-specific worry and anxiety. This means that you aren't worried about something particular, but you are in a constant state of anxiety. and You may even suffer from panic attacks that have no obvious direct cause. You may find yourself worrying about things more than necessary. You may constantly think about and plan what will happen in the future.

GAD makes worries and fears dominate your thinking and your life. It inhibits you from realizing your goals and adopting healthy behaviors. Diagnosing GAD can be difficult. After all, it is perfectly normal and even helpful to think about a future event and consider what you can do to make it successful. Thinking about future events is a good way of reducing fear and planning what to do make us more confident. The difference between GAD and healthy thinking is only a matter of degree. If you believe that you may suffer from GAD, you should seek help from a qualified medical practitioner.

People who suffer from GAD are subject to a constant barrage of worrying and intrusive thoughts that they cannot slow or control. They find themselves trapped in cycles of negative thoughts, fearing change or uncertainty. They find themselves overwhelmed by sudden feelings of anxiety and even dread which they cannot control or explain.

GAD is very common. Most studies shown that, for example, over 3% of the population (over seven million people) in the United States suffer from GAD, with women twice as likely as men to be affected. GAD develops gradually and can be caused by environmental factors and stressful life experiences. GAD manifests in similar ways to overthinking but may also cause an increased heart rate, rapid breathing, perspiring, trembling, and digestive problems.

GAD is not a mental illness. Some people use drugs to reduce its effects, but this disorder can also be improved by adopting the habits of positive thinking.

Overthinking and OCD

Another disorder that is commonly associated with overthinking is obsessive-compulsive disorder (OCD). Like GAD, this is often characterized by excessive worry, but it manifests differently. People suffering from OCD may feel that they have to perform certain actions in order to remain safe. Sometimes, these are at least relatively rational, such as frequent hand washing due to a fear of germs and dirt. Sometimes they have no objective basis at all, such as a compulsive need to count all the blue objects when they enter a room or a need to touch certain objects in a particular order before they leave a room.

What all OCD behaviors have in common is that the person suffering from them believes that acting in a certain way will have a particular effect. They may believe, for example, that touching an object a certain number of times before leaving home ensures that they will be safe during a journey. Objectively, they know that the two things are not related, but they feel compelled to complete the ritual and feel anxiety, worry, or even panic if they do not.

Just like GAD, the severity of OCD is a matter of degree. Most people have habitual behaviors, rituals that they complete without conscious thought. Checking that the front door is properly locked before leaving home, for example, is something that many of us do even though we don't need to. We have locked the door hundreds of times before and we know when it's secure, but still, we try the door after locking it, just to be certain. These behaviors become a problem when they start to affect our behavior and interactions with other people. They also become a problem when we experience feelings of panic when we are not able to complete these actions.

Overthinking and insomnia

One of the most crippling effects of overthinking is chronic insomnia. Insomnia is defined as a problem with sleeping that lasts for one month or longer. Chronic insomnia is a serious problem. It can cause an increased risk of:

- Stroke
- Seizures
- Weakened immune system
- Diabetes
- High blood pressure
- Heart disease

The fatigue that results from insomnia can leave you more at risk of having an accident, and it can make you more prone to mental disorders including anxiety, confusion, and depression. Of course, insomnia does not just originate in overthinking. Stress, worry, and even factors like diet can all affect sleep, though these tend to trigger acute episodes of insomnia that last for only a night or two.

Overthinking is associated with chronic insomnia, particularly onset insomnia and maintenance insomnia. Onset insomnia means that you have difficulty in falling asleep. When it is caused by overthinking, this often means that, no matter how tired you may feel, when you close your eyes and try to sleep, your mind starts racing. You may find yourself focusing on negative thoughts and worries about the future. In maintenance insomnia, you may find yourself suddenly awakening from sleep, often feeling anxious and worried, though your sleeplessness may not have a specific cause. When you are awake, you find it very difficult to get back to sleep.

Both types of insomnia are equally harmful. If your insomnia is caused by overthinking, using the techniques of positive thinking will help you to sleep better. You will find tips for dealing with insomnia in Chapter 9.

Chapter 3: Training Your Inner Critic

We all have an inner critic, that little voice inside your head that provides a running commentary on your life. However, if that inner critic is relentlessly negative, it can make it much more difficult to adopt the techniques and habits of positive thinking. This chapter explains the role of your inner critic, helps you recognize the messages it sends, and offers ways of changing what it is telling you.

What is your inner critic?

Your inner critic is a term used to describe the internal monologue that we all experience. It's sometime called an inner voice that speaks to us, and it is especially active in judging what we have done. Our inner critic loves nothing more than to dwell on a failure or setback. It will endlessly tell us that things went wrong because we just weren't good enough. Left unchecked, our inner critic can leave us lacking self-confidence and doubting our own ability.

The term inner critic is generally used in popular psychology. It is not a formal, academic term. In some ways, the inner critic is similar to the Freudian concept of the superego, a mental narrator that acts as a mediator and encourages behavior that accords with social norms. The inner critic is generally much more negative. This nagging inner voice will question everything we do, dwell on failures, and undermine accomplishments. Even seemingly confident and successful people can suffer from this inner critic, leaving them with unwarranted feelings such as guilt and inadequacy.

Do you remember the example from Chapter 1 of a situation where you take a test and score 90%? The inner critic is the part of your brain that, instead of celebrating your accomplishment, will focus on obsessing on how you managed to lose that last 10%. Happily, it is possible to re-train your inner critic so that this constant voice is healthier and less destructive.

Inner critic vs. inner nurturer

The inner critic isn't alone inside your head. You also have what some psychologists call an inner nurturer. This voice is the opposite of the inner critic. It praises our accomplishments and provides encouragement and self-compassion. The problem is that the voice of the inner critic is often much louder, overcoming what the inner nurturer tells us.

When these two inner voices are out of balance in favor of the inner critic, we become fearful of making mistakes. We avoid taking action because of this fear. But action is the only route to success and learning. If we become so dominated by our inner critic that we are afraid to try anything new or to take a chance, our lives are diminished. Over time, our self-confidence is eroded and our willingness to strive is seriously undermined.

How can you tell if your inner critic has overwhelmed your inner nurturer? Try asking yourself these questions:

> **Do you ever get unreasonably angry at yourself?** Think about the circumstances. Was this anger really warranted? If another person had done what you did, would you have been as angry with them?

> **Do you ever yell at yourself inside your head, telling yourself that you're an idiot or simply no good?** Again, try to step back and think about the situation objectively. Were you really acting in a way that was stupid or irresponsible?

> **Do you ever tell yourself that you are a bad or worthless person?** These are common messages from an active inner critic. Most of the time, they simply are not true.

Your inner critic has unrealistically high expectations, and it always seems ready to point out that you are not living up to these expectations. Where does this insistent and negative voice come from?

Dealing with shameful trauma

For many people, a relentlessly negative inner critic often stems from past experience, and particularly trauma. Trauma is an emotional response to a distressing situation or event. This can be an event that involved you directly, something you witnessed, or even something that you just heard or read about (this is called *"vicarious trauma"*). The response to trauma differs from person to person. For some people, the impact of trauma can be long-lasting (chronic trauma) and it can cause a number of problems including overthinking, anxiety, and insomnia. It can also amplify the effect of your inner critic.

The traumatic event(s) may be long in the past, perhaps even in childhood, and you may not even realize that you are being affected by that trauma. A common response to trauma is to feel that you could somehow have prevented the situation that led to the trauma. Often that view is false, but feeling this way can lead to emotions including intense guilt. This kind of trauma is known as *"shameful trauma."*

Traumatic events vary in intensity and duration. They can range from single acts of violence or sexual abuse or assault to what seem on the surface like longer-term but lesser traumas. For example, a consistently unsupportive and negative parent can cause trauma. What initiates the shameful trauma is not important. What matters is how it affects you. To reduce the impact of such trauma, the first thing you need to do is to consciously address the trauma. To help you achieve this, you may want to use the second exercise in Chapter 9, *Creating a trauma narrative.*

The impact of trauma may restrict your ability to think positively by increasing the power of your inner critic. For some people, the voice of that inner critic may originate in trauma.

If you listen carefully, you even may be able to identify the voice of your inner critic as a voice from your past. It may be, for example, the voice of an unsupportive parent, a competitive sibling, or a strict and judgmental teacher. Listening to the voice and recognizing the trauma from which it comes can all help lessen its effect.

Often, trauma is rooted in childhood experience. One effective way of addressing this is to write a letter to yourself as a child. You will find guidance on how to do this in Chapter 9.

.

Overcoming deceptive brain messages

Your inner critic isn't the only part of your mind that can generate confusing and unhelpful messages. Sometimes, we fall into habits of thinking that are unhelpful or even harmful. In psychology, this pattern is known as Hebb's Law. When brain nerve cells are activated in the same pattern repeatedly, they eventually form a fixed neural circuit. The more this circuit is used, the stronger it becomes. In other words, when you repeatedly react in a certain way to a particular stimulus, that reaction eventually becomes fixed within your brain. It becomes something you do without conscious thought.

This pattern leads to the formation of habits. These habits can be powerful drivers of behavior. For example, if you react to stress by eating high-calorie foods, something known as *"comfort eating,"* then your brain may make a direct association between stress-relief and eating. When you feel stress, your brain tells you that the appropriate response is to eat more. This association can become part of an unhealthy lifestyle.

Leading research psychiatrist Jeffrey Schwartz[10] describes the fixed brain circuits that can lead to unhealthy and unhelpful behaviors as *"deceptive brain messages."* In addition to causing physical behaviors, such messages can also lead to inappropriate emotional responses. Your brain may become trapped in a pattern of negativity, leading you to assume that you will fail in whatever you try to do.

The good news is that these unhelpful patterns of thinking can be replaced with a more positive approach. Your brain is capable of change through plasticity. Simply by regularly adopting the techniques of positive thinking, you can change your habitual response from negative to positive.

For more information about self-directed neuroplasticity and Jeffrey Schwartz' four-step approach, read our book about Mental Toughness.

---

[10] Schwartz, Jeffrey M, and Gladding, Rebecca. *You Are Not Your Brain: The 4-Step Solution for Changing Bad Habits, Ending Unhealthy Thinking, and Taking Control of Your Life.* Avery, 2011.

Learning to understand and master your emotions

Feeling emotional is a key part of being human. We all feel emotions, no matter how calm and collected we may seem on the outside. A problem for many people is that they do not really understand their own emotions except in the most superficial way. They recognize when they feel afraid, shameful, or angry, but they do not understand where these emotions come from or what triggers them. However, successful people who live fulfilling lives learn not only to recognize their own emotions, but they also use this knowledge to ensure that those emotions don't guide their decisions.

Within psychology, the ability to fully understand one's own emotions is measured by something called the emotional quotient (EQ). Just as the intelligence quotient (IQ) is used to assess cognitive ability, EQ is used to measure a person's ability to recognize and deal with their own emotions. EQ is a complex topic, but it is mainly concerned with developing emotional self-awareness.

Self-awareness is the first and most important step towards mastering your emotions. Emotional self-awareness may sound simple, but it isn't. We often brush aside emotions, becoming so used to them that we no longer notice our reactions. Self-awareness means learning to recognize your own emotions. It also means being able to separate out different emotions and see where they come from and what causes them. Emotions are rarely simple. They are usually made up of complex sets of feelings that interact to provide a generalized emotion. People with high EQ are not only able to recognize their own emotions, they are able to separate them out.

For example, you recognize that you feel dread anticipating a forthcoming job interview. If you look more closely, you may realize that dread comes partly from fear of failure. That fear may really be about not wanting to disappoint your family or a particular person. You may feel jealousy, and believe that a colleague who is also interviewing is more likely to get the job. You may feel anxious because you don't feel that you have all the skills you need to do the job. You may feel apprehensive because you have a history of disagreement and conflict with the interviewer.

Fully understanding the elements that comprise an overall emotion reduces the impact of that emotion. If you go into that job interview feeling fearful, anxious, angry, jealous, and apprehensive, you are very unlikely to perform well. If you understand how you feel and why, that clarity allows you to self-manage your emotions. Learning to understand your own feelings also makes you more empathetic. Empathy allows you to understand the feelings of others and see how those emotions affect their behavior.

If your actions are governed by feelings that you barely recognize, you will make decisions based on fear, jealousy, etc. These will rarely be positive of helpful decisions. To become a positive thinker, you must learn to understand and be aware of your own emotions.

For more information and exercises about learning to understand your own feelings, please see our book about Mental Toughness.

Listening to your wise advocate

We have spoken at length about your inner critic, that negative inner voice that seems to undermine everything you set out to do. Now, it's time to learn how to boost the influence of your inner nurturer, the inner voice that is actually helpful and supportive.

In their bestselling 2011 self-help book *You Are Not Your Brain: The 4-Step Solution for Changing Bad Habits, Ending Unhealthy Thinking, and Taking Control of Your Life* [11], psychiatrists Jeffrey Schwartz and Rebecca Gladding coined a new term for an improved version of the inner nurturer. They called this the *"wise advocate."* Jeffrey Schwartz later collaborated on a book solely about this topic[12], and the *"wise advocate"* has become a widely accepted concept used in promoting mental wellbeing.

The purpose of the wise advocate approach is simple: It is intended to boost your inner nurturer and to overcome negative messages from your inner critic.

This technique begins with visualizing a person. Your wise advocate can be a relative (living or dead), a real living person you have never met, or a historical figure. It can even be a character from fiction. The person should be someone you can visualize in great detail and whose intelligence and knowledge you respect. This imagined person must have integrity, and honesty, and, most important of all, they must be committed to what is best for you.

The more detailed your visualization of this person, the better. How are they dressed, how do they speak, where are they? The heart of this technique is simple: Imagine having a conversation with that person. You can describe a situation that is causing you concern or simply ask them for

---

[11] Schwartz, Jeffrey M, and Gladding, Rebecca. *You Are Not Your Brain: The 4-Step Solution for Changing Bad Habits, Ending Unhealthy Thinking, and Taking Control of Your Life*. Avery, 2011.

[12] Jeffrey Schwartz, Josie Thomson, Art Kleiner, *The Wise Advocate: The Inner Voice of Strategic Leadership*, Columbia Business School Publishing, 2019.

guidance or reassurance. They are always there and willing to chat. Listen to the advice they give.

This technique is an excellent way of becoming more objective about situations and feelings that may be confusing, and complex. Imagining the advice that an intelligent, supportive person might give allows you to step back from the situation and see it more clearly. It also helps to reduce the effect of your negative inner critic.

Creating your own wise advocate is an important step towards becoming a positive thinker. Start building the image of your wise advocate now. Try asking for them for advice, reassurance, or guidance. Start small, and use your wise advocate to address minor problems. When you become comfortable with using this technique, you will find that you can apply it effectively to many aspects of your life.

Chapter 4: The Positive Thinking Mindset

So far we have mainly looked at the elements of positive thinking and issues that may prevent it. Now, it's time to start considering how you can bring these concepts together to build the mindset you need.

However, before you begin, pause for a moment to consider what you have learned so far.

- Have you assessed your current mindset and identified problem areas?
- Do you fully understand the benefits of positive thinking? Changing your mindset is not easy, and you will need to keep the benefits in mind to provide the motivation you need.
- Do you suffer from overthinking?
- Is your inner critic a problem and do you understand the past traumas that make it more powerful?
- Do you suffer from insomnia or any of the other physical manifestations of negative thinking, overthinking, or a lack of self-esteem?
- Have you created a wise advocate to help boost your inner nurturer?

Only if you are confident that you understand where you are now and what you need to do should you think about building the mindset you need. If you are not certain, go back and read the relevant part of the first three chapters and reflect.

How positive thinking can change your life

"The positive thinker sees the invisible, feels the intangible, and achieves the impossible."

Winston Churchill

Your thoughts determine how you feel about your life. Happiness and contentment are not objective conditions that exist externally. They are present only within your own mind. If you are not happy, the answer is not to try to change your environment or simply to buy more possessions. Advertising tells us that the items we own define what other people think of us. It implies that if we own the right items, we will be happy. This is not true. It has been said that life consists of 10% what happens to you and 90% of how you think about that. Even if your life is filled with wonderful people and precious possessions, you may still find yourself being negative. If you want to become happy and to find fulfilment, you first need to address how you think. That is why positive thinking is so important.

"In order to carry a positive action, we must develop a positive vision."

The Dalai Lama

Studies show that positive thinking may even help to fight illness. A paper presented by Professor Leslie G. Walker (Chair of Cancer Rehabilitation at the University of Hull) at a British Psychological Society conference in 2000 noted that cancer patients taught relaxation and positive thinking techniques experienced a better quality of life. However, they also developed more of the white blood cells needed to fight the disease.

"Pessimism leads to weakness, optimism to power."

William James

Positive thinking doesn't just improve your physical health. It helps you to achieve what you want out of life. The most consistently successful people visualize what they want and then devise ways of achieving that. Visualizing this positive outcome makes them happy. When you visualize something that makes you happy, your brain releases endorphins, which give you a generalized feeling of well-being. This effect is just as powerful as actually doing something that makes you happy, and it reinforces your sense of wellbeing and encourages the positive mindset.

"Wondrous is the strength of cheerfulness, and its power of endurance - the cheerful man will do more in the same time, will do it; better, will preserve it longer, than the sad or sullen."

Thomas Carlyle

Becoming a positive thinker will not guarantee that you are never unhappy, nor will it automatically bring success or wealth. However, it will bring more contentment than you thought possible and it will help you to achieve your goals. It will also boost your self-confidence and improve your self-image. Positive thinking is also contagious! Think about how you feel when you spend time with someone who is optimistic and confident. You also feel your emotions being boosted until you too feel happy and positive.

"Keep my behaviors positive. Behaviors become my habits. Keep my habits positive. Habits become my values. Keep my values positive. Values become my destiny."

Mahatma Gandhi

The most successful people take chances. They see potential opportunities and are willing to take the risks needed to turn these into reality. Positive thinking will not only allow you to take chances with confidence, but it will also enable you to face your fears. Positive thinking will even allow you to deal constructively with failure if it all goes wrong.

Positive thinking can change every part of your life for the better. Some people would claim that learning to think positively is the single most significant change you can make in your life.

Are you ready to welcome all the great things that positive thinking can do for you?

Flexibility vs. rigidity

The one thing certain about the future is that it will bring surprises, some welcome, some less so. The rate at which the world is changing in terms of technology, culture, and society can seem bewildering. We must learn to be flexible, and to adapt to these changes if we are to thrive in our personal and professional lives.

Fortunately, our brains are very good at what is sometimes called "elastic" thinking. Consider the difference between a human brain and a computer. The computer is completely governed by algorithms that define how it will respond in any given situation. The computer cannot think beyond the algorithms with which it has been programmed.

The human brain is not like that. It is capable of making intuitive leaps that are beyond the capacity of any machine. It harnesses insight and non-linear thinking to generate creativity, to see what may be possible as opposed to being concerned only with what exists now. A computer can plot the most efficient route from your home to your place of work. A computer could not have invented the automobile because it lacks the ability to see beyond the present.

Positive thinking encourages and supports flexibility. It reduces fear, including fear of the unknown, and allows us instead to see opportunities in uncertainty and change. The combination of positivity and flexibility is a powerful tool in a world that seems subject to constant change.

How can you develop a more flexible approach? Begin in small ways.

> **Consider your own attitude towards change.** How do you feel, for example, if you have plans for the weekend. Then another person changes their mind, meaning that those plans no longer apply? Do you feel resentful, angry, frustrated, exasperated? Make a conscious effort instead to see the positive side: What can you do with that time that you unexpectedly have? Can you do something that will bring you even more pleasure? Try to apply this technique every time an unexpected change makes you feel irritated.

How often do you try something entirely new? That doesn't just mean something dramatic and exiting like trying skydiving or snowboarding for the first time. When was the last time you went to a restaurant or coffee shop you had never visited before? When did you last go to a new museum or art gallery? When did you try taking a completely different route to work? When did you go somewhere new for a walk? Do you always read the same newspaper or view the same on line news service? Do you always go out with the same group of people? Do you always order the same coffee or the same meal? We all tend to fall into patterns of behavior that mean we do the same old thing, time after time. It feels comfortable and safe, and the idea of doing something different can seem a little scary. Make a conscious effort every single week to experience something new, no matter how small.

Do you have a fixed routine for your days and weeks? Do you do the same things in the same order all the time? Try mixing things up a little. Go to the gym on a Tuesday instead of a Thursday. Go for lunch earlier or later. Watch a movie on a Sunday evening instead of Saturday. Each week, make the effort to vary your routine in some way.

On their own, these changes may seem trivial. But they help to acclimatize you to becoming more flexible in your thinking and they foster a more positive approach to change. Once you develop this skill, you can apply it just as successfully to the bigger changes that life is likely to throw at you.

Reaffirming your life values and goals

We all have core values, the things that matter deeply to us. Most of us also have goals that we are working towards. However, for many people, these get submerged by the flood of demands that come with everyday life. We lose touch with those values and our goals become vague and more short-term. They focus on our day-to-day life, not our hopes and aspirations for the future. Those values and goals are what should sustain us through adversity. The most successful people have clearly defined goals and values, and they spend time thinking about how they can achieve those objectives. It's time to get back in touch with what matters to you.

Let's start with personal values. In simple terms, these are the characteristics and behaviors we value. We try to attain in our own lives and we appreciate them in others. If we behave in accordance with these values, we feel good. If we behave in ways that deny these values, we feel bad. For example, let's say that one of your core values is kindness. You find yourself in a group of people who are being unkind to someone. If you speak out and try to stop that unkindness, you will feel good about yourself. If you say nothing and let that behavior continue, you will feel bad about yourself. It really is that simple.

However, identifying your core values is more difficult than you might imagine. These are also entirely personal. One person might value security and calm while another will be motivated by a desire for adventure and excitement. There is no right or wrong answer here, this is about you and your feelings.

Write a list of what makes you feel good. This can be really anything: Circumstances, situations, people, even movies and television shows. You may want to describe a recent situation that make you feel happy or proud. Focus on positive emotions.

Now, write a list of things that make you feel unhappy, angry, or frustrated. Again, be creative. Are there recent news stories that made you angry, or movies or television shows that you really didn't enjoy? Are there people you just don't like spending time with? Is there a recent situation that made you feel embarrassed, guilty, or even ashamed?

Use these two lists to produce a condensed list of what made you happy. Try to reduce these to single positive words like kindness, integrity, generosity, courage, perseverance, honesty, or intelligence. For example, if you watched a movie that left you feeling good, think about the attributes and actions of the characters that made you feel that way. What qualities did they display? Now, make a list of the things that make you unhappy. Again, aim for single words like selfishness, dishonesty, hostility, betrayal, or egotism. Again, try to identify the qualities involved, whether they were yours or someone else's.

Now you have two likely opposing lists. If honesty is in your list of qualities that make you happy, most likely dishonesty is on the other list. Use these lists to compile a single list of your core values, the things that matter most to you. You may want to come back to the lists if you think of new things to add to them. You may even be surprised at the things that make you happy.

Sometimes, our personal values can get lost in the frantic rush of life. Positive thinking means taking the time to rediscover our core values and then acting in accordance with those. Keep the list, use it as a reminder and try always to act in the right way.

Now that you have identified your values, it's time to think about goals. Goals are the things you want to achieve and are linked to values. However, while values are generally innate, you must create your own goals.

What do you want to achieve in the next month? The next six months? The next year? The next five years? Most of us have aspirations, but these are often vague and undefined. Having clear goals is important and helps you stay positive. Positive thinking will help you attain your goals. But how do you decide what your goals are? Goals are intensely personal. They are the achievements that matter to you, not to anyone else. Only you can decide what your goals are, but to be effective, goals must be SMART.

SMART is an acronym used in the world of business to ensure goal setting is effective and leads to positive change. It stands for:

Specific. The more specific a goal, the more easily you can see what you need to do to work towards it. Don't set a goal like: *"I'm going to get a better job."* Specify precisely what job or jobs you are looking for. Then, you can see what experience or qualifications you will need to get that job. The more specific your goals, the more likely you are to be able to achieve them.

Measurable. Goals only work if you can tell when they have been achieved. For example, a goal such as *"I want to be happy"* is not helpful. Everyone experiences periods of happiness and unhappiness. There is no way to tell when you have reached a particular level of happiness, and you will never reach a point where you no longer experience unhappiness. Focus instead on goals which, at any point in time, you can say whether you are still working towards the goal or you have achieved it.

Achievable. Never confuse dreams and goals. Goals are achievements that you have the ability, knowledge, and physical attributes to attain. Dreams are vague hopes that are often unattainable.

Realistic. As above, don't set goals that you lack the ability to achieve. Achieving goals may require learning and development, and that's good. But having a goal of becoming a pro basketball player if you are five foot three inches tall is never going to lead to anything but disappointment.

Timed. The most effective goals have a defined point by which you intend to achieve them. If you set a time for your goals, you will stay focused and are less likely to procrastinate.

There is one final thing to consider here: your goals should always be positive. That is to say, they should not be about avoiding failure but about attaining success. For example, *"I don't want to be fat any more"* is not a positive goal. *"I will become healthier and achieve my target weight"* is. Language is important in maintain positive thinking. You will return to these goals often, so make sure they are written in a positive way.

Create a list of goals. Aim to have at least four: One you will attain within the next month, one within six months, one within a year and one within five years. This isn't easy so take the time to get a list of goals that really motivate you. Have as many as you want, but not so many that it's difficult to remember all of them. Create the habit of regularly reviewing your goals. Do this as often as you wish. Assess what progress you have made and plan how you will make additional progress in future.

If you'd like to know more about goal-setting, you'll find detailed guidance in our book on Mental Toughness.

Mindfulness and meditation

Overthinking is something you need to learn how to overcome if you are to learn to thin positively. A very effective way of addressing overthinking is called mindfulness. The word originates in Buddhist teaching and is often linked with the practice of meditation. However, you don't have to be a Buddhist to meditate or to find mindfulness.

Mindfulness is a complex topic, and you will find several books devoted entirely to this subject. Briefly, mindfulness is about learning how to focus on the present moment and to reduce your overthinking. It teaches that worrying about the future is pointless and feeling guilt or regret for the past is simply a waste of energy. If you give your entire attention to what you are doing right now, the future will take care of itself, and you will be better able to place past events in a proper perspective. Many successful sports stars have used mindfulness to improve their performance. Executives increasingly use this technique to improve their ability to focus and to escape the stresses of their busy lives. Once you learn to do it, mindfulness can be incredibly liberating and calming, and you can do it even while doing mundane tasks like walking or even washing the dishes.

Mindfulness is often associated with meditation. Some people use meditation to find mindfulness. However, there are a number of misconceptions about meditation that may stop you from trying this approach. People associate meditation with people in loin cloths spending hours in the lotus position. They also often think it's a little odd. These assumptions are wrong. Anyone can learn to meditate. It doesn't take long, and it can be done at any time, in any outfit, and any comfortable position.

Many people also assume that meditation involves sitting for long periods thinking about nothing. That isn't true either. The central tenet of meditation is learning to listen to your inner voice and to make a conscious effort to slow down your frantic mind. To meditate, find a place where you won't be interrupted and a comfortable position. You can stand or sit, or you can even walk. The position doesn't matter as long as it is comfortable and will not distract you.

Close your eyes and relax. The first time you do this, you will probably find a barrage of thoughts competing for attention. To still these, you can use one of several techniques. One of the simplest is to focus on your breathing. Silently count each time that you inhale and exhale. Try to focus on each breath. Other thoughts will come and go. Don't worry, that's normal. Just let them come and go. If you find yourself following a particular train of thought, disconnect by refocusing on your breathing.

That's really all there is to it. Some people find it easier to use the Buddhist technique of imagining yourself as a swinging door. As you inhale, it swings one way. As you exhale it swings the other. Visualize the door and use that to focus your meditation. There are many techniques for meditation. Experiment to find what works best for you. At first, you may want to meditate for just five minutes. As you get more experienced, you may want to do it for longer.

Although it sounds simple, meditation has been shown to bring many benefits. A study carried out by Yale University found that meditation reduces activity in the default mode network (DMN), the part of the brain associated with overthinking. In 2014, Dr. Madhav Goyal and a team of researchers from John's Hopkins University carried out a research study on the effects of meditation on depression. Their findings were startling: Meditation was as effective as anti-depressant drugs at reducing the effects of depression. A 2011 study by Sara Lazar, Ph.D. at Harvard University found that meditation can change the size of certain areas of the brain. Subjects were given just eight weeks of Mindfulness-Based Stress Reduction (MBSR) training. Brain scans showed that this led to an increase in parts of the brain associated with learning, memory, and emotion regulation. The study also found reductions in the size of parts of the brain responsible for anxiety and fear.

Even better, other studies have shown that meditation can effect rapid changes. A study published in *Psychological Science*, the journal of the Association of Psychological Science, in 2013 found that just two weeks of meditation produced noticeable results in terms of improving memory and concentration and reducing overthinking. Many people report improvements in stress levels and concentration within two weeks to one month.

Try making meditation part of your daily routine. Start with five minutes, at least three days each week (or every day if you have the time). Keep this up for one month and see if you can feel any difference. In Chapter 9 you will find several exercises you can use during meditation that are specifically intended to boost positive thinking. These are:

- A loving-kindness meditation
- Mindful movement
- A week of gratitude

Use these exercises as part of your meditation routine.

How fear is holding you back

Fear is a perfectly normal emotion and one that is intended to keep us safe. However, fear of physical hazards is relatively rare. We are most likely to fear intangible things like losing the respect of others or self-respect. This can lead to a compulsive fear of failure. That too is normal: No one wants to fail when they set out to do something. But if you allow the fear of failure to stop you from trying, you will never achieve your goals.

Fortunately, there a number of effective techniques for dealing with fear.

One of the most common is called *"facing your fear."* This entails thinking through the roots of a particular fear. For example, perhaps you would like to start a new business, but you are prevented by the fear that you might fail. If you start to examine that fear in detail, you'll find that it comprises lots of subsidiary fears. You may fear losing the respect of friends, family, and colleagues. You may fear that you won't have enough money to provide for your family. You may simply fear looking silly if you fail.

Facing your fears means deconstructing your fear to look at it in detail. For example, is the fear of losing the respect of your family really rational? Would their respect increase from your willingness and ability to start a new business, whether or not it is ultimately successful? Similarly, is the fear of not having enough money to provide for your family based on fact? If you start a new business and it fails, wouldn't you be able to get another job? If you think fears through in detail like this, you will often find that they are groundless, or that you can take action to ameliorate them. If you can deal with the lesser fears one by one, you will find that the greater fear that is blocking you from taking action also diminishes.

Another effective technique is called *"pre-mortem."* This is similar to facing your fear, but it involves taking individual fears and looking in detail at the worst that could happen, then working backwards to see how you can avoid that. Take the fear of not having enough money if you start a new business. The very worst that can happen is that you find yourself penniless, homeless, and in debt. Now, think about how you might have got there and, most importantly, how you could avoid that situation. Perhaps you should have set limits on both your spending and borrowing, had more frequent reviews of your financial situation, and perhaps asked for financial advice. If you then build these things into your plans, you can be certain that you will avoid that worst-case scenario.

Perhaps the best way of dealing with a fear of intangibles is to adjust your attitude towards failure. If you want to be absolutely certain of avoiding failure, there is only one way: Never try anything and never take a chance. However, you are very unlikely to achieve your goals by following such a course. Instead, if you want to improve your life, you must be willing to take chances. Sometimes, those will mean failure. But you must learn to regard failure as not a disaster but an opportunity for learning.

Every time you fail, you learn. If you try again, that learning makes you less likely to fail again. Often it is only by trying, failing, learning, and moving on that we make real progress. Just remember the old gambler's adage: Never risk more than you can afford to lose.

.

One thing at a time

Changing your mindset to accept and use positive thinking involves many different elements and has applications throughout all aspects of your life. There is a temptation to multitask, to try and do lots of things at the same time. Don't be tempted to do this. Multitasking is almost always less effective than working sequentially, one thing at a time.

Multitasking is something that is often identified as a virtue in the modern world. It sounds practical. We all have competing demands for our time and energy. Doing several tasks at once feels like an efficient way to spend our time. Most studies emphatically show this isn't true. Multitasking produces more activity, but researchers have suggested that multitasking can actually reduce your productivity in any task by as much as 40%.

In one 2009 study[13], a Stanford University researcher, Clifford Nass, discovered that habitual multitaskers were significantly worse at picking out important information from irrelevant details. These habitual multitaskers were also ineffective when they were presented with a single task. It seemed that constant multitasking had somehow lessened their ability to identify what was really important.

These studies show that working sequentially, performing one task and staying with it until it is finished, is always more effective than trying to do several things at once.

When you are planning to introduce positive thinking into your life, work sequentially. Don't attempt to add positive thinking to everything you do at once. Make a plan. Decide where specifically you want to incorporate positive thinking. Start in small ways. Apply the new techniques, see how they work and how they change your thinking. Only then think about expanding positive thinking to other areas.

Take it one step at a time.

---

[13] Ophir E, Nass C, Wagner AD. *Cognitive control in media multitaskers.* Proceedings of the National Academy of Sciences of the United States of America, 2009

Where are you now?

It is important that you are clear about where you are right now in terms of positive thinking. You should already have completed the positive thinking assessment in Chapter 9. If not, do so now.

That assessment will confirm your current emotional style and identify three areas in which positive thinking will make the greatest difference. Perhaps there are elements of your work where you seem stuck in patterns of negativity? Perhaps you have relationships (or one particular relationship) based on negativity?

Where you choose to begin is up to you. It all depends on which life areas you want to make changes. Once you have identified three areas, look at these in more detail. Are there particular behaviors you want to change? Are there particular projects or meetings at work where you find it difficult to speak up and maintain a positive outlook? Are there personal situations where you find yourself being consistently negative?

Refer back to your values and your goals. Often, negativity is a result of acting in ways that do not accord with your values or lead to progress towards your personal goals. What do you need to do to change your behavior to match these values and goals?

Consider whether fear is making you negative. Often, we don't act or speak out simply because we are afraid. This may be a fear of conflict. It may be a fear that, by saying what we really think, we will lose the respect of other people or make them unhappy or even angry. Use the techniques for mastering fear to understand and counter your fears.

Only once you are certain where you are now can you decide where you want to begin using the techniques of positive thinking.

If you would like to know more about learning to assert your own emotions and needs, please see our book about Assertiveness.

Developing a positive self-narrative

The way in which we think about our life experiences is called a self-narrative. These are the stories we tell ourselves about our failures and successes. Try to think about one example of each from your life. Write down a brief summary of both.

Now really examine how you thought about those. How did you tell the story of your success? If that was a success at work, did you really acknowledge your hard work, dedication, and accomplishments? Or did you brush those aside and instead attribute success to luck or happenstance? Unfortunately, that is what many of us do. Complete the *Celebrating your accomplishments* exercise in Chapter 9 to focus your thinking.

Now consider your failure. Did you attribute the failure directly to your own inability, inaction, or even incompetence? This is also very common. However, the truth is that other people's action or inaction is often a contributory factor. Most failures are not entirely attributable to ourselves, yet that is how we see them.

Can you see how this fairly typical self-narrative is overall negative? You assume that success is due to outside influences yet you embrace failure as belonging entirely to you. We learn these styles of personal narrative early in life. Often, we minimize our role in success because doing otherwise is seen as boastful or selfish. This is a fundamental mistake. If you are to become a positive thinker, you must learn to reframe your self-narrative to become both positive and supportive to yourself.

Research carried out by Northwestern University[14] and published in the *Journal of Experimental Social Psychology* suggested a new way of building positive self-narratives: Competence-building narratives. This approach involves making a conscious effort to examine both successes and failures in a different way.

---

[14] Brady K. Jones*, Mesmin Destin, Dan P. McAdams, *Telling better stories: Competence-building narrative themes increase adolescent persistence and academic achievement*, Journal of Experimental Social Psychology, 2018.

For successes, you should think about how your competence, skills, experience, and hard work led to that success. Imagine if you had lacked any of those attributes. Would you still have achieved success? For failures, think specifically about the effort you put in. Then, consider that you were able to deal with the failure and, most importantly, think about what you learned from that experience that will help you to avoid the same situation in the future. If you think of them in this way, both successes and failures can contribute to positive thinking.

Go back to the example of a failure and a success that you selected above. Apply the techniques of the competence-building narrative to review them again. retell both stories in a positive way. Does that change how you feel about that success and failure?

Learn to apply this technique consistently. Don't just gloss over success and wallow in failure. Create a narrative for either that is the story of what you achieved and learned. If you do this regularly, it will become a habit. Naturally incorporating competence-building in your self-narrative is an effective and proven way to boost positive thinking.

There is always something to learn

Becoming a positive thinker will boost your self-confidence. However, you must always be on guard for confidence becoming arrogance. No matter how much you learn and how great your successes, there is always more to learn. The most consistently successful people are not just confident enough to achieve their goals, they have sufficient humility to accept that there is always room to improve.

Some people confuse humility with weakness and uncertainty, but that is a mistake. Humility is about recognizing that no person can ever know everything and that, no matter how many goals you achieve, there is always new learning available.

Positive thinking will make your happier, more fulfilled, and healthier. It cannot make you prefect. Never lose sight of that and do not be tempted to compare yourself to other people. That is something we all do, but it is not helpful or productive. Know your own inner values and be clear about your own goals. Measure your progress not against other people, but by how far your actions align with your values and advance your goals.

Toxic positivity

You now understand that positivity has all kinds of physical and mental benefits. It's a mindset that can change your life for the better. However, psychologists have come to recognize something called "*toxic positivity*" that can actually be harmful. Let's take a look at toxic positivity and how you can avoid it.

One of the main causes of toxic positivity is the belief that, in order to remain positive, you must never feel unhappiness, anger, frustration, or any other negative emotion. People who are trying to become positive thinkers can experience feelings of guilt and shame when they try to deny negative emotions. Unfortunately, you will almost certainly face setbacks and failures in your life no matter how positive you are. When you are faced with stressful circumstances, it is entirely normal to feel worried, anxious, or even angry.

Don't try to suppress or ignore these emotions. But don't dwell on them either. Accept them, then move on, using self-care and positivity to help you see the steps you need to take to improve the situation. Positivity does not mean that you will never face challenges or experience negative emotions. It simply gives you the tools to deal with these.

Another aspect of toxic positivity is ignoring problems, both your own and the problems of others. Some people seem to feel that being positive means only seeing events and circumstances that are positive, and developing a kind of selective blindness for anything negative. If you ignore your own problems, they will only get worse. Pretending that everything is fine when it clearly isn't is not positive thinking, it's just a way of hiding from reality. Accept your problems and use positive thinking to understand what is causing them and find the best way to take action to deal with them. If other people express difficult emotions, don't ignore or try to minimize these and don't try to dismiss that person with glib, superficial advice such as "*Just stay positive!*" Use positive thinking and your listening skills to be supportive and to find ways of improving the situation.

Being a positive thinker does not mean that you will never experience negative emotions. Being happy is a choice, but making that choice does not mean that you will or should be happy 100% of the time. Accept this and you will avoid the worst potential pitfalls of toxic positivity.

Chapter 5: Tools for Building Positive Thinking

Focus on your values and goals

In the last chapter, we looked at establishing what your personal values were and setting goals that align with those values. How can you use those goals to foster positive thinking?

When you are faced with making a decision, use your values and goals to help you decide. Make a decision that accords with your values and, when possible, advances your goals. If you use these criteria, you will make more positive decisions.

Make a habit each night, as you settle down to sleep, of reviewing your progress towards your goals during the day. Celebrate your successes. Consider actions you have taken that accord with your values, no matter how small.

If you suffer a failure or a setback in making progress towards your goals, use a competence-building self-narrative approach to consider what you learned from that experience. Think about how that learning will help you to succeed in future. Never allow a failure to lead you to give up on a goal. Instead, use that failure to understand how to make more effective progress.

Goals are not something that you set and then forget about. Do review your goals frequently. Lives and circumstances change, and a goal that seemed all-important 12 months ago may be less important now. If they are going to provide the motivation you need, your goals must be relevant to your current situation. Update goals as required.

Use meditation

In the previous chapter, we discussed meditation and how this can help to develop mindfulness, a state of mind that helps build positive thinking. How can you introduce meditation and mindfulness into your daily routine?

Try to set time aside for meditation. It doesn't matter where you do this provided you won't be disturbed. Remember, you can meditate for as little as five minutes or for whatever length of time you have available. Studies have shown that as little as two minutes of meditation can lead to measurable improvements in stress-reduction and mental wellbeing.

Set out a time in your daily schedule for meditation. This can be first thing in the morning, in the evening, or even during the working day provided that you find a time a place where you are comfortable and you won't be interrupted.

Remember that the purpose of meditation is not to focus on positive thoughts. The ideal meditation doesn't focus on any thoughts at all. However, simply the absence of stressful or negative thoughts gives a notable boost to positivity.

If you find it helpful, use guided meditation. These use the voice of a teacher and sometimes music to lead and deepen your meditation. Just enter *"positive guided meditation"* into any search engine and you will find many freely available on-line examples. Experiment until you find what works best for you.

Use the RAIN technique

This technique was first developed by Buddhist teacher and co-founder of Vipassana Hawai'l, Michele McDonald and further developed and adapted by psychologist and author Tara Brach, Ph. D[15]. The RAIN technique is linked to mindfulness and is intended to increase your positivity by reducing the impact of distressing or negative thoughts. RAIN is an acronym and it stands for:

- Recognize
- Accept
- Investigate
- Not-identify

If you are struggling to deal with negative emotions, you can use the four steps of the RAIN technique as follows:

Recognize. Take the time to identify the separate emotions that are troubling you. Make a mental list. Don't try to label these as positive or negative, just spend time really understanding where your current feelings are coming from. Many people find this first step helpful because it can help to untangle what may be a complex web of emotions.

Accept. Don't try to suppress emotions, even if they are negative. Simply accept that they exist. That isn't always comfortable. It may even be unpleasant. However, the first step towards dealing with emotions is simply accepting that they are there.

Investigate. Ask yourself questions about the emotions you have identified. Have you felt this way before? Can you see what caused this emotion to begin? Can you see any action that will help to reduce this emotion? Try to do this not as an interrogation, but as if you are having a friendly, supportive chat

---

[15] Tara Brach, *Radical Compassion: Learning to Love Yourself and Your World with the Practice of RAIN*, Penguin Life, 2019.

with yourself. You may even want to visualize discussing these emotions with your wise advocate as described in Chapter 3.

Not-Identify. Accept that negative emotions are a part of you, but like all emotions they are fleeting and will soon pass. Think about what compassionate action you can take to lessen the emotion and its effect on you.

Use self-care rituals

Self-care is integral to the development of positive thinking. Try to make self-care part of your daily routine. That is what is meant by a *"ritual."* You will find lots of ideas for self-care in this book. Choose that work for you and make time for them every day.

Try to make time for:

Self-compassion. Try to end each day by thinking about your accomplishments. Perhaps as you lay down to sleep, think back over the day and identify events that have made you feel happy and fulfilled. Think about actions that accord with your values and help make progress towards your goals.

Relaxation. What helps you to relax? Do you enjoy reading? Watching television? Taking a walk? Listening to music? Relaxation is important, so make sure you include time for your chosen form of relaxation in your daily schedule. Don't try to do this while you are doing other activities. If you enjoy listening to music, for example, don't do this while you are working. Make the time for just you and the music.

Grounding. Meditation is a great way of staying grounded, getting back to basics. Try to include meditation in your daily schedule, even just for five minutes.

Exercise. When your body feels refreshed and invigorated, your mind is more likely to be clear and stress-free. Try to include exercise in your daily schedule. That doesn't necessarily mean going to the gym or doing any form of intense exercise, but it should at least involve a gentle walk every day. While you are walking, take the time to really be aware of the world around you and appreciate what is happening to each of your senses.

Have a mindful conversation

Most people have conversations all the time, but the truth is that many of these conversations are ephemeral and convey little real meaning. People speak to us, but we don't really give what they are saying our full concentration and we do not respond appropriately. We may seem to be paying attention, but we are thinking about other things. Effective communication is essential if you are to understand other people and practice the skills you need to make them understand you. The ideal conversation is a mindful conversation, one in which you are fully present in the moment. You don't just hear what the other person is saying, but you really listen to them and understand their meaning. Try these steps to have a mindful conversation:

Remove distractions. Turn off your phone, if there is a computer, television, or radio in the vicinity, make sure they are turned off. Make sure you can chat freely and without interruption or being overheard. As far as possible, ignore distracting thoughts during the conversation and give all your attention to what is being said.

Look at the other person. What does their body language and posture tell you about their emotions? Make frequent eye contact, but don't stare.

Listen to the other person's voice. People communicate not just through the words they choose but through the tone of their voice. People sometimes say one thing while they mean another. Does the other person's tone of voice match their words? If not, think about why that might be.

Learn to respond, not just to react. All too often, when we aren't really listening to what another person is saying, we react to what they say with meaningless interjections: "*Hmm,*" "*Really?*" "*Wow.*" When you are listening with all your attention, when the other person pauses, you will be able to respond clearly. This lets the speaker know that you have been following what they are saying and that you understand their meaning.

Think about the speaker, not yourself. Often when we are having a conversation, we don't listen properly to the other person because we are mentally rehearsing what we will say when it's our turn. Make an effort not to do this. Remain focused on what they say. When they pause, take a moment to think about what you will say and then respond.

Are external circumstances affecting the conversation? Is the other person experiencing emotions that affect what they are saying? Are you able to recognize those emotions? Can you see where they come from? Are you able to match your responses to the other person's emotions?

Feel without judgement. Be certain that you understand what the other person is saying but respond without being judgmental or defensive. What emotions does the conversation generate in you? Can you recognize these? Do you understand where they come from? Don't allow your emotions to dominate the conversation. Be aware of them and then let them go.

You will be amazed at how great a connection you can have through a mindful conversation. You may also be surprised by how much the other person appreciates this. So much of the conversation we have every day actually involves very little communication. A genuinely mindful conversation makes everyone involved feel more positive.

How to deal with overthinking

If you suffer from overthinking, here are some techniques you can use:

Be aware of your overthinking. Just being aware that you are overthinking is a good way to reduce its effect. Overthinking is often related to the past or the future. We find ourselves endlessly reviewing past experiences and wondering what we could have done differently. Or, we find ourselves excessively worried about the future, trying to predict what will happen and focused on potential negative outcomes. Thinking about the past is only helpful if you consider what you have learned and how you can use that knowledge in the future. Any other negative thoughts about the past are unhelpful and unproductive, and you should make a conscious effort to avoid them. Thinking about the future is only useful if you are considering what you will do, i.e., if you are focused on actions and solutions.

Be solution focused. It is possible that you may face problems in the future. However, many people find themselves obsessing about a whole range of things that might (or might not) happen. This focus leads to anxiety and increases the fear that may block you from acting. Don't waste your time and mental energy on thinking about problems that may never occur. If you know about a future problem, then by all means think about what you can do to solve the problem.

Challenge your thoughts. Imagine this scenario: You are on your way to an important meeting. You are stuck in heavy traffic and you know that you are going to be late. That This situation is a prime catalyst for overthinking and imagining all the bad things that may happen. Stop. Take a deep breath and instead, challenge your racing mind. Think instead about what action you can take to improve the situation. Can you call ahead to say that you will be late? Can you reschedule the meeting? What will you do if you arrive late? Ask your wise advocate for advice. Imagine that it was not you but a friend in this situation. What would you advise them to do? Don't allow your anxiety to take charge. Refocus your thinking on the positive action you can take.

The problem with overthinking is that it is not just exhausting, it is unproductive. Overthinking generates more anxiety, and provokes more overthinking in a cycle of worry that rarely leads to positive action.

Food and mood

"You are what you eat" is one of those old sayings that modern science has proven to be true. When you are feeling depressed or just negative, it's all too easy to find yourself eating lots of ice cream or binging on high-calorie foods. Unfortunately, eating the wrong food can make you feel even more negative.

No one food causes negativity. However, A 2014 study published in the scientific journal *Brain, Behavior, and Immunity* analyzed data from a health study on nurses and found a direct link between depression and eating a diet that was high in sugar, refined grains, and red meat. Another study published in the *European Journal of Nutrition* also identified a possible link between eating lots of meat and depression.

Fortunately, there are foods that have the opposite effect. Patricia Chocano-Bedoya, visiting scientist in the Department of Nutrition at the Harvard T.H. Chan School of Public Health, has conducted a number of studies over several years and reported in an interview for Harvard Medical School that:

> *"There is consistent evidence for a Mediterranean-style dietary pattern and lower risk of depression."*

What is a Mediterranean diet? This is a diet that is rich in fruit, vegetables, olive oil, whole grains, and lean protein such as chicken and fish. This diet is also low in red meat and unhealthy fats. We also know that green vegetables such as spinach and kale contain healthy omega-3 fatty acids as well as magnesium, which appears to play a significant role in improving brain function and lifting mood.

The evidence is clear. High fat, high-sugar foods, and excessive consumption of red meat tend to depress your mood. Eating a Mediterranean diet won't just make you healthy. It will help boost your ability think positively.

Exercise

Physical exercise has been proven to be a great way to fight negativity. In addition to improving your physical health and fitness, exercise provides a number of mental boosts. When you exercise, your body releases chemicals called endorphins. These chemicals provide an immediate feeling of wellbeing as well as an energized and positive mindset. Studies have shown[16] that even a short burst of exercise can reduce feelings of anxiety and depression, boost certain cognitive functions, and help you to sleep better.

However, exercise has also been shown to have long-term effects on your brain. Several studies confirm that people who undertake regular moderate-to-vigorous physical activity perform better in academic and neuropsychological tests, particularly tests that measure mental processing speed, memory, and executive function. Physical activity also helps avoid the cognitive decline that comes with age and lowers the risk of degenerative conditions including dementia and Alzheimer's disease.

How much exercise do you need to undertake to see improvements in wellbeing? That depends partly on how intensely you exercise. The more demanding the exercise you undertake, the less time you need to spend on it to see positive results.

Recommendations from the U.S. Department of Health and Human Services suggest that for adults, the optimum is 150 to 300 minutes each week of moderate-intensity physical activity, such as brisk walking. Studies seem to indicate that exercising for 30 minutes, three times a week is the minimum required, though some people report that just 15 minutes of aerobic exercise undertaken every day can make a significant difference.

The truth is that many of us currently get little or no exercise, so any improvement at all will provide some benefit. Take the stairs instead of the elevator, park further from your place of work, get off the bus or train

---

[16] *Physical Activity Guidelines for Americans*, 2nd Edition, U.S. Department of Health and Human Services.

a stop earlier than usual and walk the remainder, or go for a brisk walk between meetings. Anything you can do to boost your current level of exercise will bring physical benefits and improve your positive thinking skills.

Affirmations

"A man is but the product of his thoughts. What he thinks, he becomes."

Mahatma Gandhi

Words are powerful. Words shape our thoughts, and thoughts direct our actions. The concept of affirmations is based on this principle. It means describing what we want to achieve in words. Speaking these words to ourselves helps direct our thoughts.

The technique of affirmation simply means finding the words to describe a positive situation you want to achieve and then repeating these words to yourself. Affirmation is not just wishful thinking. A number of studies show[17] that affirmation actually helps to rewire your brain, making us believe in these ideas and that we can achieve them. Think of affirmations as exercises for the brain. If you regularly undertake the same physical exercise, your muscles will get bigger and better at that exercise. If you repeat the same affirmation, your brain will learn to incorporate this belief in everything it does.

Affirmations are personal. They must be relevant to your life and applicable to your situation. They come from both your values and your goals. You may want to use the list of affirmations below as a starting point for creating your own.

- I am in control of my life.
- I have all the attributes necessary to succeed.
- I choose to be happy.
- I am grateful because my life is filled with plenty.
- My future will be as I plan.
- I am filled with energy and joy.
- I am focused on the present moment.
- My thoughts are positive.

---

[17] J. David Creswell, Janine M. Dutcher, William M. P. Klein, Peter R. Harris, John M. Levine, *Self-Affirmation Improves Problem-Solving under Stress*, National Science Foundation, 2013.

- I am confident and willing and able to assert my needs.

Develop a list of affirmations that are positive and relevant to you. Repeat these to yourself several times each day.

Making time for fun

Some people think of relaxation and fun as being somehow selfish and self-indulgent. They are not. In fact, they are important elements of developing a positive mindset and great ways of rewarding yourself and celebrating your accomplishments. What are your hobbies now? What do you do to relax? When you are building your daily schedule, remember to include time for both activities.

Have you ever wanted to try building a model kit, sewing a quilt, or learning how to paint? Perhaps you'd rather learn to play a musical instrument, become part of a sports team, or join a dancing class? Why aren't you doing those things?

Hobbies are affirmational and many can be mindful. They provide a complete distraction from the pressures and stress of day-to-day life and can be a source of pleasure and learning. Anything that gives you pleasure (provided that it doesn't harm you or anyone else) is positive. Don't worry about looking childish or stupid. You-time is about you, not about what anyone else thinks. Make sure that you include time for relaxation and fun in your daily schedule.

Chapter 6: The Power of Gratitude

Gratitude is a powerful antidote to negativity. All of us have things to be grateful for. Sometimes, all we need to do is refocus our thinking to acknowledge this.

How grateful are you?

Most of us have things we take for granted. We don't think about our good health until we become ill. We don't think about the fact that we have a job that allows us to provide for our families until we worry about losing it. We don't think about the fact that we live in a safe place until we see a news report from a country blighted by war or famine.

However, gratitude is not only something that helps to make us more positive. A number of studies have shown that it also improves self-esteem and relationships[18], banishes self-pity, reduces anxiety and depression[19], makes us better decision-makers, and even helps us to sleep better[20]. Fortunately, gratitude, just like the other elements of positive thinking, it is something that can be learned.

Take a moment to ask yourself how often you feel grateful. Every day? Now and again? Never? Many of us fall into the trap of never feeling grateful. We talked earlier about negativity bias, the tendency to focus on bad things and spend less time thinking about good things. You can help to offset this by consciously making the effort to think about the good things in your life.

Gratitude is something that can be entirely internal. You may feel grateful for your good health or even for something like the weather. But you may also feel gratitude towards other people in your life. How often do you express that gratitude?

This would be a good time to complete the *Reasons to be grateful* exercise in Chapter 9.

---

[18] Nezlek, John B. Newman, David B. Thrash, Todd M., *A daily diary study of relationships between feelings of gratitude and well-being*, The Journal of Positive Psychology, 2017.

[19] Fuschia M Sirois, Alex M Wood, *Gratitude uniquely predicts lower depression in chronic illness populations*, American Psychological Association, 2017.

[20] Marta Jackowska, Jennie Brown, Amy Ronaldson, *The impact of a brief gratitude intervention on subjective well-being, biology and sleep*, Journal of Health Psychology, 2015.

Start a gratitude journal

To make gratitude a habit, you may want to begin a gratitude journal. Journaling, or writing down a daily log of your feelings, has been shown to improve feelings of wellbeing. Keeping a gratitude journal boosts positive thinking. If you keep a daily gratitude journal, this helps to overcome your negativity bias and keeps you thinking positively.

The precise form that this journal takes is not important. You may want to jot things down in a notebook or create a file on your computer or phone. You can buy gratitude journals that are commercially produced for this purpose. It doesn't matter what you choose as long as you write the things you are grateful for. The simple act of writing actually changes the way you think. Writing down your feelings allows your subconscious to let them go as well as helping you to clarify what you feel. When you take the time to write something, you may discover that you actually have quite different feelings about it. Neuropsychologists have also identified the *"generation effect,"* which demonstrates that people remember more clearly material they have generated themselves compared to what they may read or hear.

Keep your gratitude journal every day. Make adding an entry to this part of your daily routine. Perhaps the journal is something you may want to keep next to your bed so you can complete it before you lay down to sleep. Perhaps you will keep it in your desk at work so that you can begin your working day with a gratitude reflection.

If there are times when you find yourself becoming negative, read back through your gratitude journal to provide an instant positivity boost.

The hierarchy of needs

Sometimes it can be difficult to find something to be grateful for, mainly because the things we should be grateful have become so commonplace that we no longer think about them. Something you may find helpful is called the hierarchy of needs, a way of defining and ranking human needs first developed by American psychologist Abraham Maslow in the 1940s.

Maslow explained that all humans have needs that fall within five categories that are ranked in a hierarchy. Only when we have fulfilled the needs in a lower category do we start to consider needs at the next level. The levels of need Maslow described are:

Level 1 Physiological. This level includes our basic needs for food and drink, air to breathe, shelter from the elements, and sleep.

Level 2 Safety. The need for an environment where we will be safe from harm, have regular employment and income, and good health.

Level 3 Love and belonging. The need for intimacy, friendship, family, and a sense of connection to a social or cultural group.

Level 4 Esteem. This includes our feelings of self-esteem and the level of respect and esteem we perceive others have for us.

Level 5 Self-Actualization. The need to feel that we have achieved all that our abilities allow and that we are able to live according to our values.

If you are struggling to find something to be grateful for, start at Level 1. Did you have enough to eat today? Were you in a place that provided shelter from the cold and rain? Do you have clothes that keep you warm? If you look through the hierarchy, you are certain to find things to be grateful for. Think about those things and how they make you feel. Think about how you would feel if you weren't able to fulfill those needs.

Everybody has something to be grateful for!

Being GLAD

If you want to boost the power of gratitude even further, you can use a technique known as GLAD. This strategy helps keep you focused on the positive aspects of your life and, if you choose, you may want to make your gratitude journal a GLAD journal. GLAD is an acronym that stands for:

Gratitude. As already described, find something to be grateful for every day.

Learning. Each day, try to identify something new you have learned. That can be through formal learning or just something that your experience during the day has shown you. For example, you may have learned the meaning of a new word or you may have learned that refusing a second cup of coffee before breakfast makes you better able to concentrate. Be creative! Every day brings learning, but we often don't notice.

Accomplishment. Most people tend to think of accomplishments in terms of major life changes, like getting a new job or passing an examination. But every day there are accomplishments you can celebrate. Did you get to work on time? Pay a bill? Remember a friend's birthday?

Delight. Did something today make you feel joyful, or did you experience something that was pleasing to your senses? Did the sunrise look wonderful? Did the crunch of snow under your boots make you smile? Was your lunch particularly tasty? Did you see a cartoon or hear a joke that made you laugh? Try to find something that improved your mood during the day.

Gratitude meditation

In general, meditation isn't about anything in particular. It's about clearing your mind of overthinking and being in the present moment. However, you can also practice meditation by reflecting on the things you are grateful for. Studies have found that using a gratitude meditation three times a week for just three weeks can lead to a substantial improvement in wellbeing[21].

You can create your own gratitude meditation. This can be about anything at all, from good health to the abundance of foods available at stores to an appreciation for the wonders of nature or the support of friends. Choose something that you feel personally grateful for and spend five to 10 minutes reflecting on this.

Alternatively, you can use a guided gratitude meditation. These are freely available on line. They consist of the voice of a teacher leading you through thoughts of gratitude. Many of these guided meditations also include soothing music which can be a simple and effective way to meditate. Simply enter *"gratitude meditation"* in any search engine and you will be presented with many options.

---

[21] Karen O'Leary, Samantha Dockray, *The effects of two novel gratitude and mindfulness interventions on well-being*, Journal of alternative and complimentary medicine, 2015.

Chapter 7: You Aren't Alone

Examining your relationships

Most of us are involved in a complex web of relationships that include family, friends, colleagues, and partners. Our mindset has an impact on our relationships, and there is no doubt that positive thinking can make you a better partner, a more supportive friend, and a more effective colleague. However, these relationships also have a direct effect on your wellbeing and especially on your capacity for positive thinking. Relationships develop slowly over time and often, we become so used to these associations that we no longer understand how they affect us. It's time to assess your relationships and look at whether they are having a positive or negative impact on your life.

There have been a number of attempts to find ways to measure relationships. Some of these methods use complex analytic methods to assess how a particular relationship impacts you. If you would like to know more about that approach, there are several helpful books available[22]. However, there is a simpler way to assess what effect a relationship is having on you. Consider spending time with a particular person. Think about the emotions that generates in you.

We all know people who are relentlessly negative. People who seem to take pleasure in complaining about their lot in life but never seem to do anything to change that. These people have not just accepted negativity bias, they seem to embrace it. How does spending time with a person like that make you feel? In general, a negative person will make you feel negative, too. They also tend to be self-centered and selfish. They will want you to listen to their negativity, but they are not interested in how you feel or what you have to say.

Do you know anyone like that?

Now think about spending time with someone who is positive. They always have lots of plans, they may make you laugh, and you leave them feeling energized and even more positive. You will also notice that these

---

[22] David Easley, Jon Kleinberg, Networks, *Crowds, and Markets: Reasoning about a Highly Connected World*, Cambridge University Press, 2010.

optimists seem to be more willing to listen to you. They are actually interested in how you feel. They may offer advice if you ask for it and give support and encouragement if you need it. Of these two kinds of people, which would you rather spend time with? For virtually everyone, the answer is that they would rather spend time with a positive person than a negative person. Negativity kills relationships. Positivity builds better relationships.

Of course, most people cannot be easily categorized as wholly positive or negative. We all have both characteristics in different circumstances. But generally, most people tend towards positivity or negativity. Think about your relationships and try to see if each is generally positive or negative.

How relationships affect you

A number of studies show that relationships have a profound effect on our mental and physical wellbeing. Social isolation (having few meaningful relationships) is bad for you. People who are socially isolated tend to die younger[23] and have less resistance to illness[24]. However, toxic relationships also have a notable impact on health. Marriages characterized by discord and conflict can lead to high blood-pressure and increased risk of heart attack and depression[25]. Negative relationships are associated with negative lifestyle behaviors and increased risk of illness and death[26].

One 2011 study[27] went even further. It concluded that:

- "Social ties affect mental health, physical health, health behaviors, and mortality risk.
- Social ties can benefit health beyond target individuals by influencing the health of others throughout social networks.
- Social ties have both immediate (mental health, health behaviors) and long-term, cumulative effects on health (e.g., physical health, mortality)."

---

[23] Berkman Lisa F, Syme Leonard, *Social Networks, Host Resistance, and Mortality: A Nine-Year Follow-up Study of Alameda County Residents.* American Journal of Epidemiology. 1979

[24] House James S, Landis Karl, Umberson Debra, *Social Relationships and Health,* Science, 1988

[25] Kiecolt-Glaser Janice K, McGuire Lynanne, Robles Theodore F, Glaser Ronald, *Emotions, Morbidity, and Mortality: New Perspectives from Psychoneuroimmunology.* Annual Review of Psychology. 2002.

[26] Umberson Debra, Crosnoe Robert, Reczek Corinne, *Social Relationships and Health Behaviors across the Life Course.* Annual Review of Sociology. 2010.

[27] Debra Umberson, Jennifer Karas Montez, Social Relationships and Health: A Flashpoint for Health Policy,

Journal of Health and Social Behavior, 2010.

In other words, positive relationships don't just make you heathier and happier. They affect the people around you in the same way. If you find yourself involved in a negative relationship, you only have two options. You can end the relationship or you can try to change it to become more positive. But how can you change a relationship?

Setting boundaries

One of the most effective ways of changing a relationship is to set clear boundaries that protect your emotional space. These boundaries are closely linked to your values. When people speak or act in ways that infringe on these values, you are left feeling uncomfortable and negative. The purpose of setting boundaries is to let others know what your values are and to allow you to enforce these.

For example, let's suppose that one of your core values is friendship. However, you have one friend who is regularly unkind to other friends, either through their actions or speech. They regularly say unpleasant things about your other friends and that makes you feel bad. You must assert your boundaries, telling that person how important friendship is to you and that you do not want to listen to unkind gossip about other friends. Each time they speak in this way, you must make the same assertion. Be clear that you are not telling them that they must not indulge in malicious gossip, only that you are not prepared to listen to it.

There are two possible outcomes. Either that person will come to accept that they cannot speak in front of you in that way, or they will no longer want to spend time with you. Either is beneficial. If that person modifies their behavior, you will no longer be complicit in a situation that does not accord with your values. If the person decides to end their friendship with you because they will not or cannot change their behavior, then that was a relationship that you will be better off without.

If you find yourself feeling uncomfortable or negative when you spend time with someone, that is almost certainly because you are not acting in alignment with your values. Setting boundaries isn't easy, but it is the only way to ensure that you can act according to your values, and that is an essential part of positive thinking.

Learning to listen

Most of us can hear, but few of us take the time to really listen. We have previously discussed mindful conversation, but the simple act of listening is a key part of successful communication. If you want people to listen to what you say, you also need to learn to listen to them. Listening is a skill that comprises three elements:

> **Attending.** Have you ever spoken to anyone who clearly isn't paying attention? Perhaps they're checking their phone while you speak, acknowledging other people, or just allowing their attention to wander. That is infuriating, isn't it? Make sure you don't do that while someone is speaking. Give them your full attention, maintain eye contact, and let them know that what they are saying matters to you.

> **Following.** Here is another infuriating attribute of poor listeners. They allow you to speak but, instead of offering support or even acknowledging what you have said, they immediately hi-jack the conversation to their own agenda. They follow what you have said with a litany of their own problems, which are always (in their perception) worse and more intense than yours. Don't make this mistake as a listener. Try to understand the emotions behind what the other person is saying and use gentle questions to get them to tell you more.

> **Reflecting.** People who are bad at listening will rarely understand what you are trying to say. To confirm that you have understood, use statements like "I think what you saying is..." to confirm that you have understood.

All relationships are about making a connection with another person. Learning to listen effectively is a key part of making that connection.

Learning to speak

Most people are able to speak, but many people find it very difficult to say what they want and need, particularly in terms of emotions. Learning to say what you want is called assertiveness, and it is a key skill for anyone who wants to become a positive thinker.

Assertiveness is not the same as aggression or arrogance. Assertiveness is about learning to state your needs while respecting the needs and views of others. This is a complex topic, but in brief, assertiveness means learning how to set boundaries, how to say *"No"* when that is appropriate, and how to give effective assertion messages that describe your needs.

Assertion messages are appropriate in any situation where you want to clearly state your own needs. Reflect on the example for the *"Setting boundaries"* section where you want to tell a friend to stop talking maliciously about other friends in front of you. In that case (and in most cases where you want to assert yourself) the use of a three-part assertiveness message works well. Such a message would take this form:

> **Describe the problem.** In the case of the example, this might take the form of: *"You are often rude about people who are my friends."*

> **Describe how that makes you feel.** In the case of the example, this might take the form of: *"That makes me feel uncomfortable."*

> **Describe how the other person's behavior affects you.** In the case of the example, this might take the form of: *"When you say those things, I feel like I have to choose between supporting my other friends and agreeing with you."*

You will note that the message simply sets out your feelings and reactions, but it doesn't propose a solution. That is because the most effective solutions are created jointly. When you first give an assertion message, the other person may become defensive or even angry. Let that pass. If necessary, repeat the message. Wait for the other person to overcome their initial emotional response and begin to examine what you say rationally. They should then offer solutions. If they don't or won't, you may have to consider whether you still want to spend time with that person.

If you would like to learn more about learning to listen, say "No" and assert your own emotions and needs, please see our book about Assertiveness.

Chapter 8: Your Positive Thinking Plan

It's time to pull everything together and develop your own personal positive thinking plan. Now that you understand how important positive thinking is and what a significant difference it can make to your life, you probably want to begin as soon as possible. That's entirely understandable. Of course, you want to realize the benefits of positive thinking right now.

But it is important that you don't rush things or try to do too much at once. Changing your mindset to become a positive thinker is not something that will happen overnight. It means building new, positive habits to replace the negative habits that may be affecting you now. You are beginning a process of change. Plan carefully, accept that it will take time, and don't be tempted to multitask. Taking one thing at a time will always be the most effective way to proceed.

Goals and values

In Chapter 4, we discussed the significance of values and goals. Their importance is worth re-stating here. These goals and values will guide you in everything you do. They will become the roadmap that will provide you with direction on your journey towards positive thinking.

Review the list of values you created in Chapter 4. Do they really accord with the things that matter deeply to you? Is there anything missing? This list is not static as it may evolve over time. Review it regularly to ensure that it covers everything that is important to you.

At least once each day, review what you have done within the previous 24 hours. Did your actions accord with your values? If not, what can you change to make that happen? Don't be angry with yourself if you sometimes act in ways that don't align with your values. Instead, think about what happened, learn, and use that knowledge to act differently next time. When you do act in ways that accord with your values, particularly where those involve difficult situations, celebrate your accomplishment by giving yourself a reward: Take some extra time for a hobby or relaxation, watch a favorite move, or make yourself a special meal.

Now, review your goals. You should have at least four goals: One you intend to attain within the next month, one within six months, one within a year, and one within five years. Feel free to have more, but not so many that it's difficult to remember them all. Between four and eight goals is ideal.

Are each of your goals:

- Positive?
- SMART (Specific, Measurable, Achievable, Relevant, and Timed)?

For some of your goals, especially those that are long-term, you will need a plan. For example, if one of your goals is to have achieved a promotion at work within 12 months, are there intermediate steps such as training or experience that will help you to achieve that goal? These will become sub-goals and they too must be SMART.

Make a plan for how you intend to achieve each goal. Tale time and provide all the details you need. At least once each week, review the progress you have made towards your goals in the previous seven days. Don't get angry or frustrated if you fail to reach your self-imposed targets. Failure is only a problem if you don't learn from it. Think about why you failed to make the progress you wanted. Was there something you could have done differently? Did you put enough time and effort into pursuing your goal? Was the level of progress you anticipated simply too optimistic? When you do make the progress you had hoped for, celebrate that accomplishment.

Daily positive thinking

In addition to thinking about your values and assessing progress towards your goals, there are other things that you can do every day to boost positive thinking.

Gratitude. Gratitude is the single most powerful antidote to negativity. At least once every day take the time to consider something for which you feel gratitude.

Meditation. Regular meditation helps to prevent overthinking and monkey mind. Try to schedule meditation, even just for five minutes, every day. Remember that you can use guided meditation to focus on a particular topic such as positivity or gratitude.

Affirmations. Repeat your affirmations to yourself several times each day. You can even set reminders on your computer to make sure you don't forget.

Self-care. Include time for relaxation and self-compassion every day.

Diet. Eating a Mediterranean diet won't guarantee positive thinking, but it certainly will avoid the sluggish, negative feelings that come from consuming high-fat, high-sugar foods. Make sure your daily diet includes as many healthy options as possible.

Exercise. Exercise boosts positivity. Try to include time every day for at least moderate exercise such as brisk walking, swimming, vacuuming, washing windows, mopping, or mowing the lawn. Aim for at least 150 minutes of moderate exercise every week but if you can increase this to 300 minutes, you will see greater benefits. If you undertake vigorous exercise such as jogging, fast cycling, playing tennis or soccer, or aerobic dancing, you should aim for a minimum of 75 minutes per week.

Measuring progress

Each day, try to take a moment to think about how positive thinking has shaped your behavior. Can you identify some situation where positive thinking has made you act in a way that makes you feel good? It can be something small, like trying a new place for lunch, giving a piece of positive advice to a friend or colleague, or watching a movie or television show that made you feel energized and positive. It can also be something big, like making a decision through positive thinking. Are you able to contrast this behavior with how you might have acted in the past, held back by negativity and a lack of confidence?

Also try to think about how positive thinking has made you feel differently each day. Has meditation made you better able to focus and avoid stress? Have your improved diet and exercise regimens made you feel stronger and more confident? Perhaps you can feel that your affirmations are working and that situations that previously made you feel fearful and negative are now less stressful?

After you have been working on positive thinking for at least one month, you may want to go back and re-take the exercise in Chapter 9, *Your positive thinking assessment.* Has your emotional style changed? Have you been able to apply positive thinking to the three areas of your life you identified in that exercise? Are you now ready to start using it in other areas?

Every single day, the habits of positive thinking are making a difference to your life. Be aware of these changes and celebrate them to keep your motivation high. Soon positive thinking will become something you do automatically.

Focusing on positive and motivational material

Every day you are bombarded with information through advertisements and promotional material. You probably also watch television and movies, listen to the radio and podcasts, and read. All this information is processed by your brain, and it directly affects your mood and positivity level. It's almost impossible to avoid advertising, but you can be selective in what you choose to watch, listen to, and read.

For as long as movies and television have existed, there have been heated debates about the potential negative effects of this media including incitement to aggression and violence, reinforcement of sexual and social stereotypes, and increasing the perception that the world is a fearful and dangerous place. However, more recent studies suggest that the media we are exposed to also has the ability to have a positive impact on us.

For example, in 2012 a study conducted by one of the leading scholars in the field of media research, Mary Beth Oliver of Penn State University[28], looked at movies that portrayed *"moral virtue,"* attributes like gratitude, generosity, and loyalty. In one study, a group of subjects were asked to identify recent movies that had been pleasurable or meaningful to them. Pleasurable movies were simply those that the subjects enjoyed watching. Meaningful movies were those that the subjects remembered intensely afterwards and which emotionally affected them. Almost without exception, movies identified as meaningful included altruistic content such as a fight for social justice or care for the weak.

Earlier research suggested that increased levels of watching television and movies led to what was identified as *"mean world syndrome,"* a feeling that the world is frightening and dangerous. However, this more recent research suggests that certain kinds of media can also lead to *"kind world syndrome,"* a much more positive view of our environment.

---

[28] Oliver, Mary Beth; Hartmann, Tilo; Woolley, Julia K., *Elevation in Response to Entertainment Portrayals of Moral Virtue*, Human Communication Research, 2012.

The implications for positive thinking are clear. If you carefully choose what media you are exposed to (and this includes what you read and listen to as well as what you watch), this practice can have a significant effect on your mindset. If you consistently choose inspirational material, this will provide a long-term boost. Consuming media is no different from eating food. If you eat healthily only now and again, that will have little overall effect on your health. However, if you make healthy eating a regular part of your lifestyle, you will become healthier. If you make a conscious, consistent choice to watch, listen to, and read uplifting material, you will boost your ability for positive thinking.

Every day, think about the media you consume. Is it supporting your desire for positivity by providing inspiration and hope? You may be fascinated by those bleak, true-crime podcasts, but the truth is that they are giving a boost to your view of the world as a mean place, Switch to other materials that help you to see the world as a kind and supportive place.

Your 30-day positive thinking plan

You have probably noticed that this section is called *"your 30-day positive thinking plan."* That might sound a little daunting. Can you really achieve positive thinking in just 30 days? Is that timeframe long enough to change your current negative mindset? The answer is that this 30-day plan is only the beginning. It is a structured way to try all the important techniques of positive thinking and to see how they work for you.

Don't worry, you don't have to complete all of these steps in 30 days (though of course you can!). You can stretch it out over whatever period you feel comfortable with. But try not to stretch it out too long. Achieving positive thinking is about establishing new habits. Habits are best formed by doing something repeatedly until it becomes subconscious. Doing something intensely for 30 days is a good way of beginning to establish new habits. However, if you want to stretch these steps over, for example, 90 days, that should still work well. If you are tempted to stretch it even further, you may want to consider whether you are really committed to positive thinking. If you feel that it will take you more than three months to tackle all these steps, perhaps you need to re-read the parts of this book that cover the many benefits of positive thinking and use these to provide the extra motivation you need.

Try not to skip any steps. All are important elements of building your positivity and self-confidence.

Here is your 30-day plan:

> **Day 1:** Write down your life values and personal goals. These are important, so don't begin until you have the time to think these through.

> **Day 2:** Take the time to give yourself an overall score for how frequently you are affected by the physical symptoms of overthinking. For each of insomnia, headaches, muscle and joint pain, and fatigue, assign a score from 1-10 with 1 being *"almost never"* and 10 being *"very frequently"*. Record your total score.

Day 3: Begin meditating. This can be for as little as five minutes ot it can be for longer if you feel that this provides additional benefit. For the remainder of the 30 days, practice meditation once every day or, if you really can't find the time for that, at least once every other day.

Day 4: Create your wise advocate. Take the time to visualize this person intensely. If you feel stressed or doubtful during the remainder of this 30-day plan, visualize a conversation with your wise advocate.

Day 5: Create your list of affirmations. Try to have at least four. For the remainder of the 30 days, repeat these to yourself at least once every day.

Day 6: Exercise. If you already exercise regularly, you can carry on with your current regime. If you don't, introduce at least 25 minutes of moderate exercise (such as swimming or brisk walking) into your daily routine. Maintain this for every day of this 30-day plan.

Day 7: Diet. Take a look at what you are eating and drinking right now. Does that include high-fat, high-sugar foods or lots of red meat? Think about how you can make the change to something more like a Mediterranean diet. You'll be keeping this up for the remainder of the plan.

Day 8: Begin a gratitude journal. Today and for every remaining day of this plan, take the time to write down at least one thing for which you feel gratitude. Try to find a different thing every day.

Day 9: Today, try something new. Take a different route to work, go somewhere new for lunch, go to a museum or gallery you have never visited before. Think about what emotions that experience made you feel.

Day 10: This is a good time to pause for reflection. By now you have begun meditating, using affirmations, and keeping a gratitude journal. You have created your wise advocate, and you have incorporated exercise and a healthy diet in your daily routine. How are these new techniques making you feel? Are you struggling with any of them? If so, you may want to go back and reread the relevant part of this book to check you are doing what you need to do.

Day 11: Today, focus on your emotions. Be aware of the emotions that affect you throughout the day and try to understand where they come from. At the end of the day, reflect on these emotions and try to see how they shaped your behavior.

Day 12: Today, try a guided gratitude meditation. Find one on line.

Day 13: Have a mindful conversation. Identify someone you want to have a deeper connection with and use your abilities as a listener to let that person know that you truly understand what they are saying.

Day 14: Today, focus on other people's emotions. Try to identify the feelings that are affecting the people around you and see if you can work out where they come from. At the end of the day, reflect on what you have observed and try to identify one person whose emotions shaped their behavior.

Day 15: Identify a situation where you are able to give an assertiveness message that sets or reinforces your personal boundaries.

Day 16: Create a competence-building narrative about your current work role.

Day 17: Identify something new that you want to learn about. Ideally, this should be something you currently know very little about. Perhaps it's a country you would like to visit, a new exercise regime you are interested in, or an author you have heard about but whose work you haven't read. Whatever you choose, start finding out about your chosen topic today and make notes about what you learn.

Day 18: Today, mix up your daily routine. Make a conscious effort to do things in a different order and at varied times.

Day 19: It's time to face your fear. Focus on a situation or event that makes you apprehensive. It can be anything at all: A job interview, a blind date, a visit to the dentist, the spider under the closet. Use the *"face your fear"* and *"pre-mortem"* techniques to explore this fear in detail. Come back to it as often as you want during the day. Look at your fear again at the end of the day. Is it less now than it was this morning?

Day 20: Another good time for reflection. Do you feel you are making progress? Have any of the things you have done in the last 20 days made a particular difference to your positivity? Did you find any of these things especially challenging? Think about why and about the emotions these successes and challenges made you feel.

Day 21: Watch an uplifting movie or television show or read a book that inspires you. Try to choose something you wouldn't normally watch or read. Choose something that includes the depiction of *"moral virtue."* How did that make you feel? Did it make you feel energized and positive? Perhaps you may want to continue focusing on uplifting material for the remainder of this plan?

Day 22: Today it's time for self-compassion. Over the last 20 days, you have been learning to apply the techniques you need to become a positive thinker. How does that make you feel? What have you learned? What have you accomplished? Particularly consider your accomplishments and give yourself a pat on the back for getting this far.

Day 23: Practice a loving-kindness meditation.

Day 24: Have another mindful conversation but this time, with a different person.

Day 25: Today is about relaxation. Whatever it is you do to relax, watching television, reading, listening to podcasts, give yourself extra time doing it today. You have earned this you-time with your hard work over the previous 25 days.

Day 26: Create a competence-building narrative about your current personal relationships.

Day 27: Go back to your values and goals. Do you feel that you are making progress towards your goals? Do you feel that your actions are now more in accord with your values?

Day 28: Focus on your emotions throughout the day. Can you see any difference from the emotions you experienced on Day 11? Are you now experiencing more positive emotions?

Day 29: Repeat the exercise from Day 2. Has the frequency of the physical symptoms of overthinking changed? What techniques of positive thinking have led to the greatest reduction in your overthinking?

Day 30: You have done it! Congratulations! You have now practiced all the techniques of positive thinking. But your positive thinking journey doesn't end after 30 days.

What's next?

That's it, you have completed the 30-day plan so you can now put aside this book and go back to how you were before, right?

No!

During the 30-day plan, you tried the techniques of positive thinking and incorporated them into your daily life. Some have now begun to become habitual. Many have yet to become embedded. Instead of stopping, this is a good time to think about what you have learned and how you plan to continue.

Which techniques worked best for you? Which provided the most significant boost to positivity? Those are the techniques and lifestyle changes that you need to incorporate in your life, not just for 30 days but from now on. Becoming a positive thinker isn't something you do just for 30 days. It's a fundamental change in how you view the world and your place in it. Pick out the things that worked well and make them part of your everyday life.

Which techniques didn't work for you? Perhaps you didn't find meditation helpful. Maybe you found that completing the gratitude journal made you feel silly. Everyone is different and not all the techniques work for every person. However, all the techniques in this book are important building blocks for positive thinking. Don't abandon those that didn't give you an immediate boost just yet. Instead, continue with all the techniques for at least another thirty days. At the end of that period, review your situation again. If some techniques just don't seem to be working, you can consider dropping them. After 60 days, many of these things will have become habits and you may find that instead, you want to continue.

Troubleshooting

What happens if you follow the guidance in this book, adopt all the tools for positive thinking, and include them in your daily routine, but you just can't shake that feeling negativity? Here is some guidance to help you get back on track to positivity.

What's the problem? Sometimes, major life-changes can affect your ability to stay positive. The break-up of a relationship, losing your job, moving to a new home, or the illness or death of someone close to you will all cause extreme negativity bias in your mindset. That's normal. Is there a situation in your life that is currently blocking you from positive thinking? Are there steps you can take to reduce the impact of that situation? If not, you may want to select any positive thinking tools that you find helpful and use those to make yourself feel more positive. But you may have to accept that, until the stressful situation passes, it may be more challenging to become fully positive.

Too much, too soon? You can see the benefits of positive thinking and perhaps you feel tempted to push things along as fast as you can? That's understandable, but it's also counterproductive. Multitasking is never as effective as working on one thing at a time. Achieving positive thinking involves establishing new habits, and there is no way to rush that. A new habit can take anything up to 90 days to become embedded in your thinking. Are you taking this fact into consideration?

Back to basics. Perhaps you missed something important? Read back through Chapters 4 and 5. Do you have a positive thinking mindset? Have you clearly established your values and goals? Do you have a flexible approach to how to support those and have you incorporated meditation in your daily routine? Have you learned to deal with overthinking? Do you practice daily affirmations? Are you getting enough exercise, and is your diet one that will help boost positive thinking?

Stamp out negativity! If you find yourself in a pattern of negative thinking, end it immediately. Begin by identifying those thoughts as negative and unhelpful. Try using the RAIN technique. Make a conscious effort to think about something else or start another activity to distract your mind. Try a short burst of exercise to boost your endorphin levels and increase positivity. Challenge those negative thoughts by discussing them with your wise advocate. If you find yourself repeatedly thinking in negative ways about a specific situation, add a new affirmation that accentuates the positive in that situation.

Chapter 9: Positive Thinking Tips and Exercises

Your positive thinking assessment

Using the information from Chapter 1 and, if you wish, an on line emotional style test, assess your emotional style.

Do this as many times as you need, answering the questions based on a particular aspect of your life, for example, at work, in relationships, in a social context, etc.

You should now be able to see where a lack of positive thinking has the greatest impact on your life.

Now, write down the three areas in which positive thinking will have the greatest impact. These are the areas you should apply the positive thinking techniques in this book. After one month, reassess. Can you see improvements? Can you now see other areas where you could apply these techniques? Always try to have a current list of the three areas where you will focus your efforts to apply positive thinking and keep assessing your progress.

Creating a trauma narrative

This exercise is about looking at a trauma that has shaped your life and changing the narrative to something that you can build on.

- Begin by identifying a trauma that has shaped your life and your emotional and behavioral response to stress. You may be able to identify more than one trauma. If so, create a separate trauma narrative for each. Write down your answers to the following:
    - Describe the trauma. Add as much detail as you can, describing your actions and those of others.
    - Describe your emotions associated with this trauma. Especially be aware of any feelings of shame, guilt, helplessness, or fear.
    - Can you identify any instances where the emotions generated by this trauma continue to affect your behavior now?
    - Write a new narrative of the trauma. Be objective and try to write this as if you were another person looking at the situation. In particular, focus on describing how you were not responsible for the events involved in the trauma.

Reviewing a past trauma can be painful. However, it is a valuable way of lessening the effect of that trauma. Be honest here and take the time to write about any past situation that continues to affect you.

A loving-kindness meditation

Loving-kindness meditation (LKM) is a widely recognized and helpful self-care technique that has been proven to reduce stress and increase capacity for connection to others.

To practice loving-kindness meditation:

- Find a time and place where you will be free from interruption or distraction. Find a comfortable position, close your eyes, relax your muscles, and focus on your breathing.
- Imagine what absolute physical and emotional wellness and inner peace would feel like. Focus on this feeling. Each time you breathe out, imagine that you are breathing out tension and stress. Each time you breathe in, imagine you are breathing in feelings of tranquility and love.
- Repeat one or more positive affirmations to yourself. These should be specifically about your wellbeing, such as:
    - I am content, healthy and strong.
    - Today I will give and receive love and respect.
    - Each day I learn and grow.
    - I am in control of my life.
- Maintain your feelings of loving kindness for yourself for a few minutes. If you find your attention drifting, redirect it back towards self-compassion.
- Now, direct your focus to the important people in your life: your family, partner, children, and friends. Feel your love for each of them in turn and consider your gratitude towards them.
- When you feel that your meditation is complete, open your eyes.

When you begin loving-kindness meditation, you may want to focus solely on yourself. When you become confident with this technique, then extend it to other people in your life. You may even want to include people you engage in conflict with. This can help with feelings of compassion and forgiveness.

The precise technique you use for this meditation is not important as long as it promotes feelings of loving kindness towards yourself and others.

Celebrating your accomplishments

Negativity bias can make it hard to recognize all that you have achieved. Instead, we often become focused on our failures. Take the time to make three lists with the following accomplishments:

Past accomplishments. Go back as far as you want. Is there something you achieved in school that you feel especially proud of? Were your examination results in college something to be proud of? Did you build a fantastic tree house for your kids when they were young? Did you help a friend or colleague through a difficult time? It's easy to forget about all the positive things we have done but it's important to celebrate those. Go into as much detail as you want and try to list at least 10 things here.

Current accomplishments. Think of both your recent work and personal life. Think of what you have achieved in your working life. The achievement doesn't have to be a huge career success. Getting to work on time every day even when you are fatigued and being a reliable and supportive colleague are also accomplishments worth noting. In your personal life, can you think of times you were a supportive friend or a loving partner, parent, or family member?

Future accomplishments. Think about what you want to achieve in the future. It may help to review your past and current accomplishments. Which of those make you feel most proud and positive? Perhaps those are the kind of achievements you want to repeat in future.

Write a letter to your younger self

Write a letter to yourself when you were a child. This should be a letter that would have empowered and energized your younger self. Don't plan too much. Just write and see what comes out. You may want to meditate to clear your mind before beginning this exercise.

In particular, address these questions:

- What positive qualities would you want to highlight to yourself as a child?
- What gratitude would you want to share?
- What achievements would you want to share?
- What fears would you want to negate?
- Can you think of one thing that you could write that would immediately make your younger self feel more positive?

Reasons to be grateful

Take the time to think about and write down something that you were grateful for today. Don't just write down the first thing that comes to mind. Really think about this and consider the positive emotions that this event made you feel. The more descriptive you can be, the more effective this approach is.

Now, try to identify four more things in your life that make you feel grateful. Again, be descriptive and note the emotions these provoke.

Mindful movement

Mindfulness is not just something that can be experienced though meditation. Many daily events can be made mindful if you approach them in the right way. The essence of mindfulness is to be entirely present in the moment and fully immersed in the information that your senses provide. Here are some examples of applying mindfulness to daily events:

Mindful walking. This method entails being aware of each step that you take and every breath. Also be aware of the world around you: The sight of sun though trees, the sound of the wind over leaves, the smell of newly cut grass, the feel of leaves crunching under your feet. Leave your headphones and music behind and don't rush. Walk steadily and calmly, immersing yourself totally in the experience. You can practice mindful walking anywhere and at any time, even as you make your way from meeting to meeting, and it is a great way to calm a monkey mind.

Mindful dance. Be aware of how the different parts of your body feel. Be aware of the sights and sounds around you. Note how the music provokes emotions in you. Lose yourself completely in the experience.

Mindful cooking and eating. When you are preparing food, be aware of how individual ingredients feel, look, and smell. When you are ready to eat, note the color, texture, and smell of the food. Savor each mouthful, appreciating all the tastes and textures. Focus entirely on the act of eating without distraction.

Mindful chores. Even something as mundane as washing dishes can become mindful. Focus on what you are doing, not what you will do afterwards. Enjoy the feeling of warm water on your hands and the knowledge that you are making those dirty dishes clean. Many chores are incredibly grounding, but we rush through them, thinking about anything but what we are doing now. That makes these chores dull and uninteresting. It doesn't have to be that way. As Zen Master and revered mindfulness teacher Thich Nat Hanh says:

"I know that if I hurry in order to eat dessert sooner, the time of washing dishes will be unpleasant and not worth living. That would be a pity, for each minute, each second of life is a miracle.[29]"

No matter what you are doing, each moment of your life has significance. Be fully present in everything you do and you can find mindfulness anywhere.

---

[29] Thich Nhat Hanh, *The Miracle of Mindfulness: An Introduction to the Practice of Meditation*, Beacon Press, 1999.

Dealing with insomnia

The effects of chronic insomnia can be crippling, and it is very difficult to be positive if you are fatigued, irritated and unable to focus. If you are suffering from acute and troubling insomnia, you may need to consult a healthcare professional. There are also many books and articles about insomnia and how to deal with it, but here are some tips that you may find useful:

Keep your bed separate from the rest of your life. Your bed is a place you should associate with sleep and intimacy and nothing else. If space permits, don't spend time sitting on your bed during the day. Don't take phone calls on the bed, and don't watch television there. If you do these things, your brain comes to associate bed with the activities of daily living rather than sleep.

Stay away from screens before and after going to bed. The screens of televisions, computers, phones, and some other electronic devices emit blue light. Our brains interpret this as daylight and inhibit the production of melatonin in our bodies, a chemical associated with sleep. Most electronic book readers such as Kindles do not emit blue light.

Establish a going to bed routine. Try to go to bed at the same time every night. Don't watch television or use electronic devices for at least one hour before you go to bed. Have a light snack and a non-caffeinated drink. Some foods such as grapes, strawberries, nuts, cherries, and oats contain melatonin and may help you sleep. Have a warm bath, which may also stimulate melatonin production. Complete your gratitude journal and meditate. Do the same things in the same order each evening to create a routine that gives your brain a cue that it will soon be time to sleep.

Listen to music or read in bed. Choose music that is soothing and relaxing. Likewise, don't choose to read anything too gripping, frightening, or exciting before you settle down to sleep. By all means read something uplifting or an old favorite.

Stay away from alcohol. Alcoholic drinks may make you feel drowsy, so some people take a nightcap to help them get to sleep. However, alcohol can affect your brain in a number of ways that may reduce sleep quality, so avoid alcohol before going to bed.

See the light. Being exposed to daylight early in the day can help to normalize your circadian rhythm, your body's internal clock that regulates when to sleep and when to be awake. If it's not possible to expose yourself to natural light early in the day, you may want to consider using a light therapy box.

Exercise. In addition to all the other benefits it brings, the energy use and body temperature changes that exercise causes can help to promote good sleep. However, avoid intense exercise for at least two hours before you go to bed because this can actually make it harder to get to sleep.

Chapter 10: Conclusion

This book provides everything you need to know to become a positive thinker. It also explains all the benefits positive thinking brings and how to turn positive thinking techniques into life habits. There is nothing mystical here and nothing based on faith. The advice in this book is drawn from current psychological and medical knowledge proven to be effective. It doesn't guarantee that you will always be happy or that you will become wealthy or famous. It does mean that you can make the best use of the abilities you already have, and it will have a positive impact on your health and wellbeing.

You now know everything you need to get started thinking positively. The rest is up to you. Only you can make the decision to improve and take action to transform your life through the power of positivity.

What are you waiting for?

If you enjoyed this book, make sure to leave a review as this would help us out tremendously!

YOUR FREE GIFT

We would like to give you a gift to thank you for purchasing this book. You can choose from any of our other published titles.

You can get immediate access to any of our books by clicking on the link below and joining our mailing list:

https://campsite.bio/mastertoday

Our other books

Mental Toughness & Discipline Mastery: *Build your Self-Confidence to Unlock your Courage and Resilience*

Build Your Self-Confidence, and Unlock Your Courage to Endure Hardship and Perform Under Any Condition!

Mental toughness will help you rise above the many people who are easily affected by their external circumstances such as challenges, obstacles, and mishaps. It allows you to perform under pressure and overcome life's challenges.

This book hands you the keys to develop true mental toughness.

Image yourself dealing with life's problems with confidence, certainty, and a lion-like courage. Picture yourself facing any issue or setback that might occur. Are you ready for that?

If yes, this mental toughness & discipline mastery book is for you!

Build your self-confidence and unlock your courage and resilience to deal with adversity... Persevere, handle the pressure, and stick to your plans. Stop draining your energy and get more out of life than you thought possible!

Toughen your mind and master your discipline, control your impulses, and endure the emotional and psychological distress that is the root cause of misfortune. Make feeling overwhelmed, exhausted, or overburdened symptoms of the past.

In **Mental Toughness & Discipline Mastery**, you will discover:

- What mental toughness is, and what it is not...
- The character traits that mentally tough people learned to rise above mediocrity.
- Why motivation and willpower are not dependable tools.
- How discipline helps you get more out of life.
- How mental toughness is the essential ingredient for success.
- The keys to strengthening your mind and unlock peak performance.
- How you can delay gratification with ease.

Become mentally tough. The book includes a step-by-step workbook and 15 powerful exercises that will help you turn what you will learn throughout this book into daily habits!

Stop giving up when life gets tough. Master your mind and discipline to become resilient. Start your training and grab your copy of this book today to face adversity with courage!

Find out more here:

https://master.today/books/mental-toughness/

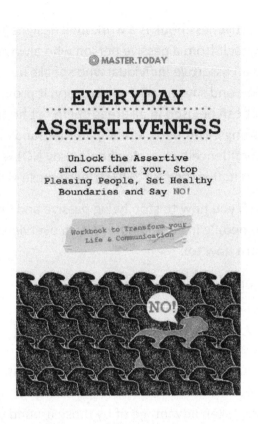

Everyday Assertiveness: *Unlock the Assertive and Confident you, Stop Pleasing People, Set Healthy Boundaries and Say NO!*

(Workbook to Transform your Life & Communication)

Do you feel like you are not assertive enough? Are you tired of people taking advantage of you?

You may be thinking, *"I don't want to offend people. I just want them to like me."* But what if they do not take the hint and never stop asking for your attention and help? What if they keep pushing and demanding more of your time, energy, or money? How will that make you feel? And how will it affect your goals and relationships with others in the long run?

The Everyday Assertiveness book is a workbook designed to help you transform yourself from a passive person who always pleases other people into an assertive individual who speaks up, sets healthy boundaries, and says no when necessary. It provides practical tools that can be used in all areas of life - at home, school, work, or social settings. This book has helped thousands of individuals gain confidence by learning how to say NO! without feeling guilty about it. It is time for YOU to learn these skills too!

This book will teach you how to stop being passive and become assertive with the people in your life. Here is an overview of the things you will learn how to:

- Be more confident.
- Stop letting other people walk all over you.
- Set healthy boundaries that work for YOU!
- Say NO when appropriate without guilt or shame.
- Get what YOU want out of relationships, friendships, family members etc.
- Stop feeling taken advantage of by those around you.
- Set boundaries and say no when necessary.
- Take full charge of your own life!

Purchase the Everyday Assertiveness workbook today!
Find out more here:

https://master.today/books

Made in the USA
Las Vegas, NV
11 February 2024